THE MAGIC OF

NORSE RUNES

Unlock the Ancient Power of the
Elder Futhark – A Guide to
Reading and Casting Rune Stones
for Divination, Spells, and Modern
Witchcraft

ERIK HANSEN

novus
liber

For permission requests, please contact:
Novus Liber Publishing
Email: info@yourbookshelf.top

First edition October 2024
Revised edition April 2026

Paperback ISBN 978-1-961963-56-6

Contents

Introduction

People come to the runes by different roads. Some grew up hearing about them from grandparents who kept the old stories alive. Others stumbled across them online or in a bookstore, drawn by something they couldn't quite name. A few, like me, found them while looking for something else entirely.

I was in Norway on one of my first trips there, tracing my family's roots through coastal villages and quiet archives, when the runes appeared. They were carved into a stone in a small museum — angular, deliberate, ancient — and I stopped in front of them longer than I'd stopped in front of anything else that day. I didn't understand them. But I recognized something in them, the way you sometimes recognize a place you've never been. That feeling never left me, and this book is, in part, the result of following it.

The runes are an ancient alphabet developed by the Norse and Germanic peoples of northern Europe. They were carved into wood, stone, metal, and bone to mark ownership, commemorate the dead, record laws, send messages, and write prayers. But alongside this practical life, they carried a deeper one. Each rune was understood as a living force — a condensed symbol of some principle in the cosmos — and carving or speaking a rune's name was thought to call that force into the world. The same marks that a merchant might scratch onto a crate could, in the right hands, become a protection spell or a healing charm. This dual existence is part of what makes the runes so enduring and so endlessly interesting.

They've survived the Middle Ages, the Christianization of Scandinavia, centuries of disuse, and a great deal of modern misappropriation, and they still speak. Today, thousands of people around the world work with runes as a tool for reflection, self-knowledge, and spiritual practice. Their power isn't diminished by the passage of time. If anything, the distance gives them a kind of clarity — they're free from the noise of the moment, rooted in something older and steadier.

Working with runes means learning to sit with ambiguity. They won't hand you a decision or tell you what to do. What they do is hold a mirror up to what you already sense — the concerns you've been circling, the fears you've been avoiding, the strengths you haven't yet claimed. The more honestly you engage with them, the more honestly they respond.

The best way I found to build that kind of engagement was simple: each morning, I drew a single rune. Then, throughout the day, I paid attention — noticing where its energy seemed to show up, sometimes literally, more often symbolically. Each evening I wrote about it: what I'd read, what I'd noticed, what surprised me. Over time, those daily pages became something more valuable than any reference book. They became a record of how the runes were speaking specifically to me, in the language of my own life.

I'd encourage you to try the same. Keep a notebook alongside this book. Jot things down — first impressions, questions, moments in your day that seem to rhyme with a rune's meaning. You don't need to have it figured out. The runes reward patience and return visits far more than they reward certainty.

What you'll find in the pages ahead is this: we start with history, tracing the runes from their earliest known inscriptions through the great arc of the Viking Age and into the Middle Ages. From there we move into Norse mythology — the gods, the Nine Worlds, and the story of how Odin won the runes through sacrifice. Then comes the heart of the book: a detailed guide to all twenty-four runes of the Elder Futhark, each one explored through its symbol, its meanings, and its relevance to lived experience. The final section turns to practice — runic magic, divination methods, and how to build a daily rune work that's genuinely your own. We close with a look at the great runic inscriptions that have survived to the present day, and at where the runes stand in the world right now.

This is a book to return to. Some sections will resonate immediately; others will open up later, after you've spent more time with the runes themselves. However you move through it, I hope it serves as a beginning — not a conclusion.

The runes have been waiting a long time. Let's get started.

The Origins: Before the Runes

E very alphabet has a beginning. For most of the writing systems we use today, that beginning is reasonably well documented — a civilization, a time period, a set of traceable influences. For the runes, the question of origin has been debated by scholars for well over a century, and no fully satisfying answer has emerged. What we have instead is a constellation of evidence: physical objects, linguistic analysis, careful comparisons between scripts, and a few tantalizing accounts from Roman writers who observed Germanic peoples from the outside. Together they sketch a picture that is not quite complete but compelling enough to follow.

The story starts, as it often does in archaeology, with a disputed object.

The Contested Brooch

In the late nineteenth century, excavations in Meldorf, in what is now the Schleswig-Holstein region of northern Germany, turned up a silver brooch — a fibula — dated to somewhere between 50 and 100 CE. On its inner surface were marks. Whether those marks are runic inscriptions or simply decorative Roman-influenced ornamentation has been argued ever since. Scholars are roughly divided. Some read the marks as a clear early example of runic letters, which would push the confirmed origin of the alphabet back almost a century further than previously thought. Others maintain that the resemblance to runes is coincidental, that the craftsman was working in a Roman decorative tradition and the marks mean nothing alphabetically.

The Meldorf fibula remains open. It may be the oldest runic inscription ever found, or it may not be a runic inscription at all. This is, in miniature, the situation scholars face across the entire question of runic origins: suggestive evidence that stops just short of proof.

The Vimose Comb

The first inscription that essentially all researchers agree is runic dates to around 160 CE. It comes from a bog deposit at Vimose, on the Danish island of Funen, where archaeologists working in the nineteenth century recovered an extraordinary collection of weapons, tools, and personal objects — a cache of war trophies, most likely, deliberately deposited as an offering. Among the finds was a small antler comb inscribed with a single word: *harja*. The word's meaning is open to interpretation. It could refer to a warrior, or it could be a personal name. What is not in question is the inscription itself, which shows a clear and confident runic hand. This was carved by someone who knew the letters well, which means the alphabet itself was already established, already in use, already — in all likelihood — old.

The Vimose comb gives us a fixed point in time. It tells us that by the mid-second century CE, at least some Germanic communities in Scandinavia were using a runic alphabet fluently enough to inscribe personal objects with it. The gap between the comb and the Meldorf fibula represents exactly the kind of contested early period that makes the runes so historically fascinating.

The Problem of Origins

The question scholars return to constantly is this: where did the runic alphabet come from? Writing systems don't emerge from nothing. They are almost always derived, at least in part, from existing models — borrowed, adapted, reimagined. The alphabet you are reading now descends from Latin, which descended from Etruscan, which descended from Greek, which descended from Phoenician. Every script carries its ancestry in its shapes.

For the runes, four main candidate scripts have been proposed. The Roman alphabet is one, given the extensive contact between Germanic tribes and the Roman Empire during the centuries when the runes were developing. Greek is another, given similarities between several runic forms and their Greek counterparts. North Italic scripts — particularly those used by Alpine communities like the Veneti and Rhaetians before Roman conquest — are a strong contender, favored by many researchers because the geographic proximity and the formal resemblances are difficult to dismiss. A fourth possibility, argued by a smaller group of scholars, is that the runes developed more independently from the Scandinavian Bronze Age tradition of rock carvings, absorbing foreign alphabetic influence at a later stage.

The North Italic hypothesis deserves particular attention because the geographic and formal evidence is harder to dismiss than for the other candidates. The Alpine peoples who used these scripts — the Veneti near present-day Venice, the Rhaetians in what is now the Tyrol, the Lepontic communities of northern Italy — were in sustained contact with Germanic tribes along the trade and migration routes that crossed the Alps. Several runic letters show striking formal resemblance to their North Italic counterparts, and the directionality of early runic inscriptions — right to left, or alternating — mirrors the conventions of these older scripts rather than the left-to-right norm of Roman writing. If the runes grew from a North Italic root, the process was not simple borrowing but a deep adaptation: Germanic communities taking a Mediterranean alphabet, stripping it of the features that didn't serve their needs, reshaping the forms to suit wood and bone, and adding a layer of symbolic meaning that went far beyond phonetic function.

No single theory has won the argument, and it is worth accepting that the answer may be plural — that runes emerged from a confluence of influences, shaped by communities in contact with multiple writing traditions, adapted over generations to serve their particular needs and cosmological understanding. The runes may have had parents rather than a single parent.

What is clear is that whoever first devised or assembled the runic alphabet made deliberate choices in doing so, and one of those choices is written into the shapes of the letters themselves.

A Script Built for Carving

Look at a runic inscription on wood or bone — or even on the recreations you'll find in museums — and notice what the letters have in common. They are angular. They use diagonal strokes and verticals. What they don't use, with very few exceptions, is horizontal lines.

This is purposeful. Wood has a grain, and a line cut perpendicular to that grain — horizontally across a staff or stave of wood — tends to blur, splinter, or disappear into the natural texture of the material. A diagonal cut, by contrast, crosses the grain cleanly and holds its edge. Anyone who has ever carved a message into a piece of timber understands this instinctively. The people who shaped the runic alphabet understood it too, and they built it accordingly.

This is one of the strongest pieces of evidence that the runes, whatever their ultimate ancestry, were not simply copied from another script. They were engineered for a specific medium. The forms were adapted to fit the hand and the material — the knife, the antler, the flat stave of wood. Even as runic inscriptions later appeared on stone, metal, and bone, the underlying angularity of the letters reflects their origin in something more portable and immediate.

Early runic inscriptions also show another feature that speaks to their antiquity: the direction of writing was not yet fixed. Some inscriptions run left to right, as English does today. Others run right to left. Some alternate direction line by line, a practice known as boustrophedon — the plow-turn, named for the way an ox turns at the end of a furrow. This variability is characteristic of very early alphabets, before conventions solidify. It places the runes in a category with some of the oldest writing systems known to history.

Tacitus and the Casting of Lots

Around 98 CE — before the Vimose comb, before any confirmed runic inscription — the Roman historian Tacitus wrote his *Germania*, a description of the Germanic tribes beyond the empire's northern frontier. He describes a divination practice that has attracted the attention of runologists ever since. A branch from a fruit-bearing tree is cut into strips, each one marked with a distinct sign. The strips are scattered at random on a white cloth. A priest, or the head of the household, then picks up three of them, one at a time, and reads the signs that have been chosen.

Tacitus doesn't name the signs he's describing. He writes in broad terms, as an outsider recording unfamiliar customs. But the practice he describes — carved marked lots, cast and read for guidance — maps closely onto what later sources describe as runic practice. Many scholars read this passage as the earliest external reference to a runic tradition, or at least to the cultural conditions from which one was already emerging.

Whether or not Tacitus was watching someone use runes, his account confirms something important: that the Germanic peoples of the first century CE had a well-established practice of using carved symbols for communication with the divine, and that this practice was integrated into the structure of their religious and social life. The marks meant something. The casting was ritualized. The reading required knowledge. Whatever alphabet those marks belonged to, they carried weight.

Period I and the Spread of the System

Scholars generally classify the earliest phase of runic inscriptions as Period I, running from approximately 150 to 550 CE. The objects that carry these inscriptions are diverse — spearheads found in North Germany, shield mounts from Funen and Sjælland and Jutland, jewelry, buckles, and personal items — but they are consistent in one respect: they all show the Elder Futhark, the oldest and most complete form of the runic alphabet, in use across a wide geographic range.

By the fifth century, the Elder Futhark had reached its settled, canonical form. The Kylver Stone, a limestone slab discovered in Gotland, Sweden, and dated to around 400 CE, carries the fullest known inscription of the complete alphabet in sequence: all twenty-four letters, arranged in their traditional order. It is the runic equivalent of a primer — the alphabet laid out as if to be read, learned, or preserved. Standing in front of it in a museum, what you're looking at is essentially a textbook from sixteen hundred years ago.

By 500 CE, the runic alphabet had traveled across the Germanic world — north into Scandinavia, south into what is now Germany, west into England, and east into territories that are today parts of Russia, Hungary, and Poland. The objects it traveled on tell a story of their own. A spearhead found at Kowel, in what is now Ukraine, carries the inscription *tilarids* — "attacker" or "goal-rider" — in Elder Futhark letters, placing runic practice deep in territory far removed from its Scandinavian heartland. A bracteate found in Denmark bears a rune sequence scholars still argue about, its meaning preserved but its context lost. Each object like these is a small proof of reach: that the alphabet was not confined to one community or one landscape but had become the shared property of a wide and mobile Germanic world.

How that transmission happened — through trade, migration, religious networks, or some combination — remains a matter of ongoing inquiry. The letters survived the journey. Their exact path did not.

The Futharks: Runes Through the Centuries

T he Elder Futhark is what most people mean when they talk about runes. It is the oldest complete system, the one used in this book, the one whose twenty-four symbols have carried meaning for nearly two millennia. But it was never the only runic alphabet, and it was not the last. Over roughly eighteen centuries — from the second century CE to the early twentieth — the runes changed, branched, contracted, expanded, and finally faded, in a history that tracks closely with the larger story of the Germanic and Norse peoples who used them. Each alphabet that grew out of the original was a response to something: a shift in language, a new geography, a different set of needs. Reading that history is its own kind of education in what writing systems actually do.

The Elder Futhark

The name "futhark" is simply the runic equivalent of "alphabet" — a word built from the first letters of the sequence. In Greek, *alpha* and *beta*. In the runic system, *f, u, þ, a, r, k*. The Elder Futhark takes its modifier from its age: it is the older one, distinguished from the Younger Futhark that eventually replaced it in Scandinavia.

The twenty-four runes of the Elder Futhark are organized into three groups of eight, each group called an *aett* — an Old Norse word meaning something like "clan" or "family." These groupings are old enough that their origin is not entirely understood, but they were clearly intentional: each *aett* has its own internal logic, grouping runes by theme and by the energies they represent. The three *aettir* will be explored in depth later in this book. For now, what matters is the structure itself, which imposed on the Elder Futhark a sense of order and relationship that went beyond simple alphabetical sequence.

Each rune in the Elder Futhark has a name. Fehu for the first rune, Uruz for the second, and so on through Othala, the twenty-fourth. These names are not arbitrary labels — they are words that carry meaning in their own right, each one pointing toward the concepts and forces that the rune was understood to embody. Fehu means cattle, and by extension wealth. Uruz means the aurochs, the wild ox, and by extension untamed strength. The name was the rune and the rune was the name; the two were not separable.

Reconstructing these names with certainty has been one of the challenges of runic scholarship, since the Elder Futhark itself predates any written record of the Germanic languages. Linguists have worked backward from later runic poems — surviving texts from the Anglo-Saxon and Old Norse traditions that catalog the runes and gloss their meanings — and from the names of letters in related alphabets, including the Gothic script. The results are not perfect, but they are consistent enough to give us a working picture of what the earliest rune-users understood their letters to mean.

Three runic poems survive that are particularly valuable for this reconstruction. The Old English Rune Poem, preserved in a manuscript that was unfortunately destroyed in a fire in 1731 though not before being copied, pairs each letter of the Futhorc with a brief verse that elaborates its name. The Old Norwegian Rune Poem and the Old Icelandic Rune Poem do the same for the Younger Futhark's sixteen symbols. None of these poems is straightforwardly transparent — the verses are compressed, allusive, and sometimes deliberately cryptic, as if the runic knowledge they contain is being shared selectively rather than published freely. But read alongside each other and alongside the archaeological record, they provide the closest thing we have to a documented runic curriculum from within the tradition itself. They are, in effect, the teaching materials of a practice that was transmitted primarily by demonstration and memorization, briefly and incompletely committed to parchment before passing out of living use.

The Elder Futhark remained the dominant runic system from its emergence in the second century CE through roughly the seventh or eighth century, when the pressures of linguistic change began to pull it apart.

The Anglo-Saxon Futhorc

When the Germanic tribes known collectively as the Anglo-Saxons crossed the North Sea and settled in Britain beginning in the fifth century, they brought the runic alphabet with them. What happened next is a good illustration of how writing systems adapt to the people who use them.

English — or rather, the family of dialects that would eventually become English — was phonetically different from the continental Germanic languages in which the Elder Futhark had developed. It used sounds that the twenty-four original runes did not adequately represent. The solution was expansion. Over time, the Anglo-Saxon runic tradition grew from twenty-four symbols to twenty-eight, and eventually to thirty-three, adding new characters to cover new sounds. This expanded system is known as the Futhorc, a name that reflects the slight shift in the pronunciation of the fourth rune from *ansuz* to a sound closer to os.

The origins of the Futhorc are themselves debated. Some researchers trace it to Frisia — the coastal region of what is now the Netherlands and northwestern Germany — and argue that it spread from there to England. Others believe it developed primarily in England and was later exported back across the North Sea. The two territories were closely connected through trade and migration, and the question of priority may not have a clean answer.

What survives from the Futhorc tradition is vivid. The Ruthwell Cross, a seventh- or eighth-century stone monument in Scotland, carries runic verses from a poem known as *The Dream of the Rood*, carved in a confident and practiced hand. The Thames scramasax — a long knife pulled from the Thames in 1857 — has all twenty-eight letters of the Futhorc inlaid along its blade in silver, an object that is both a weapon and an alphabet. Runic manuscripts survive from this period as well, including the so-called Cotton Otho codex, a runic poem that catalogs the Anglo-Saxon letters with brief verses on each one. The Futhorc was a living system, used for inscription, literature, and seemingly for the same range of purposes — practical, commemorative, and magical — as the Elder Futhark before it.

The Marcomannic Runes

One branch of the runic tradition is less well known and considerably more curious. In the eighth or ninth century, a group of Carolingian scholars — working in the southern Germanic territories of what are now Bavaria and Alemannia — produced an alphabet by combining elements of the Elder Futhark and the Anglo-Saxon Futhorc. Their goal was systematic rather than practical: they wanted to create a rune for every letter of the Latin alphabet, a one-to-one correspondence that would allow the two scripts to be mapped onto each other.

The result is described in a Carolingian treatise called *De Inventione Litterarum*, attributed in some manuscripts to Hrabanus Maurus, a Frankish scholar and theologian. The alphabet it describes has come to be called the Marcomannic runes — a somewhat misleading name, since the Marcomanni were a Germanic tribe from an earlier period who had nothing to do with its creation. The name stuck anyway, carried forward by scholars who had already attached it before the attribution was corrected.

The Marcomannic runes are a scholarly artifact more than a living script. There is little evidence that they were used for everyday inscription. They represent, instead, a moment of intellectual effort: an attempt to preserve and systematize runic knowledge at a time when the Carolingian world was absorbing and cataloging the traditions of the peoples it encompassed. They are runes seen through a Latin lens.

The Younger Futhark

The most significant development in the history of runic writing after the Elder Futhark is also, on the surface, the most counterintuitive. Sometime around the ninth century, the runic alphabet used across Scandinavia shrank. The twenty-four symbols of the Elder Futhark were reduced to sixteen. The Younger Futhark, as it came to be called, dropped eight runes and carried on with what remained.

The puzzle is this: the Old Norse language of the Viking Age was phonetically more complex than the Proto-Norse of earlier centuries. It had more distinct sounds, more vowel distinctions, more nuance in its consonants. By any logic of utility, the alphabet should have grown to keep pace. Instead it contracted, with the result that single runes now had to cover sounds that had previously been distinguished. The letter that had represented one consonant now did service for two or three.

Scholars have not settled on a satisfying explanation for this. Some suggest that the Younger Futhark developed in a context where speed of carving mattered more than phonetic precision — where a simplified set of forms was more practical for the range of purposes runes served in daily Viking Age life. Others argue that the reduction was driven by aesthetic or ritual considerations that are no longer recoverable. A third possibility, raised less frequently but worth considering, is that the contraction reflects the increasingly special-ized nature of runic literacy in this period: not everyone needed to write with full phonetic accuracy, and a reduced alphabet served the majority of practical purposes well enough that the complexity of the Elder Futhark was shed as unnecessary weight. What we can say with confidence is that the people who used the Younger Futhark were not confused by it. They understood how to read and write it, navigating its ambiguities in the way that all experienced readers navigate the ambiguities of any writing system — through context, convention, and the knowledge that certain sounds in certain posi-tions were more likely than others.

The Younger Futhark comes in two regional variants. The long-branch runes, associated primarily with Denmark, have fuller, more elaborate forms. The short-twig runes, used in Sweden and Norway, are more compressed, their strokes reduced to a minimum. The distinction likely reflects different carving traditions rather than fundamentally different systems, and the same runic content could be — and was — written in either variant. In practice, skilled carvers appear to have moved between the two with some freedom, the choice of form shaped by available material, personal habit, and the context of use as much as by strict regional convention.

Medieval Runes

By the twelfth century, the contraction of the Younger Futhark had begun to reverse. Medieval rune-users started adding new symbols to handle the phonetic distinctions that the sixteen-symbol system had collapsed, gradually rebuilding something closer to the full range of the Elder Futhark, though with forms influenced by centuries of separate development.

This later, expanded system coexisted with the Latin alphabet in a way that the earlier futharks never had. Christianity had brought Latin literacy to Scandinavia, and from the eleventh century onward, runes and Roman letters were used side by side — sometimes in the same inscription, sometimes by the same hand. The two scripts were not rivals so much as tools for different registers of communication. Latin carried the weight of the church, of official record, of learned writing. Runes carried the everyday.

The Bryggen inscriptions, discovered from the 1950s onward in Bergen, Norway, make this ordinary life extraordinarily vivid. Bryggen was a medieval harbor district, and beneath its later construction layers, excavations uncovered more than six hundred runic inscriptions carved on wooden sticks and bones — a number that has grown with subsequent digs. The inscriptions are not monuments or memorials. They are messages. Names and addresses. Commercial transactions. Complaints about unpaid debts. Declarations of love. Prayers for help, sometimes in Latin, sometimes in Norse, sometimes in both. One stick carries an inscription that translates, roughly, as: "I love another man's wife so much that fire seems cold to me." Another appears to be a simple shopping list. Taken together, the Bryggen material rewrote the scholarly understanding of medieval runic literacy. Runes were not the exclusive province of carvers and commemorators. They were a script that ordinary people used to write to each other.

The Dalecarlian Runes

The last chapter of runic writing played out in a remote corner of Sweden. In the province of Dalarna — geographically isolated, culturally conservative, its valleys separated from the surrounding landscape by geography that made outside influence slow to arrive and slower to take hold — a local runic tradition persisted long after the alphabet had disappeared from the rest of Scandinavia. The Dalecarlian runes, which blended traditional runic forms with influences from the Latin alphabet, were in active use from the sixteenth century onward and were still being written by some residents of the region as late as the early twentieth century.

Their primary use was for writing Elfdalian, a North Germanic dialect so distinct from standard Swedish that it is sometimes classified as a separate language. Elfdalian preserves phonological features that disappeared from other Scandinavian languages centuries ago, and the community that maintained it did so alongside their own script — a combination of cultural conservatism and geographic isolation that together preserved something that would otherwise have been absorbed and lost. In a community that maintained its own language and its own script, the runes functioned less as a mystical inheritance than as a practical tool, the way people there wrote things down and had always written things down, without particular ceremony around the fact.

What makes the Dalecarlian tradition remarkable in retrospect is not its mystical dimension but its sheer persistence. The runes survived in Dalarna not because anyone was deliberately preserving them as objects of reverence but because they remained genuinely useful for a community that had its own language and its own needs. When they finally faded — and their disappearance in the early twentieth century coincides with the broader integration of Dalarna into modern Swedish life, with improved roads and compulsory education and the radio — it was not because a tradition was suppressed but because the practical conditions that had sustained it changed.

The Dalecarlian runes are, in a sense, the longest surviving thread of the runic tradition as a living writing system. By the time they fell out of active daily use, the runes had been in continuous practice, in one form or another, for roughly eighteen centuries. That is a long life for any alphabet.

The Viking Age: The World That Used the Runes

H istory has not been entirely fair to the Vikings. The word itself — which refers specifically to those who went on sea raids, not to the whole of Norse society — has become a shorthand for a kind of uncomplicated ferocity: horn-helmeted warriors pillaging monasteries, leaving ruin behind them before vanishing back into the North Sea. That image contains a sliver of truth and loses almost everything else. The people who produced the runic tradition were farmers, merchants, poets, craftspeople, explorers, and lawmakers, as well as raiders. They built towns and maintained complex legal systems. They navigated open ocean by the stars and reached North America five centuries before Columbus. They argued cases before the *thing*, the assembly at which free men settled disputes through debate rather than violence. And throughout all of it, they wrote.

The period scholars call the Viking Age runs roughly from the late eighth century to the end of the eleventh — from the first recorded Scandinavian raids on the British Isles in the 790s to the Norman Conquest of England in 1066, or by some reckonings to the Christianization of the last holdout Scandinavian kingdoms around 1100. These three centuries represent the moment when Norse culture reached its widest geographic extent and, not coincidentally, when the runic tradition was at its most visible and most diverse.

A World in Motion

The Viking Age was defined by movement. Scandinavian peoples fanned out across the known world along routes that were, by the standards of the time, staggering in their reach. Norse settlers colonized Iceland in the ninth century, Greenland in the tenth, and reached the coast of North America — at the site now known as L'Anse aux Meadows in Newfoundland — around the year 1000. In the west, Norse kingdoms took root in Ireland, Scotland, and northern England, and Viking rulers sat on the English throne in the early eleventh century. In the east, Scandinavian traders pushed down the great river systems of what is now Russia and Ukraine, establishing the Kievan Rus' and opening trade routes that stretched as far as Constantinople and Baghdad. To the south, Viking mercenaries served in the Byzantine emperor's personal guard, the Varangian Guard, and left runic graffiti scratched into the marble of the Hagia Sophia — an inscription that reads, simply, *Halfdan carved these runes.*

Runes traveled with all of this. Wherever Norse people went, the practice of runic inscription went too — carved into objects they carried, cut into stones they raised, scratched onto surfaces they passed through. The geographic distribution of runic finds maps almost exactly onto the routes of Viking expansion, making the corpus of runic inscriptions a kind of accidental atlas of the medieval Norse world.

Who Could Read Them

One question that scholars have long debated is how widely runic literacy was distributed in Viking Age society. The older assumption — that runes were the specialized knowledge of priests or professional carvers, inaccessible to ordinary people — has been substantially revised in light of the archaeological record. The range of objects bearing runic inscriptions is simply too broad, and too mundane, to support a picture of runic knowledge as rare or elite.

Weapons, yes — swords and spearheads bearing protective inscriptions were common. But also combs, spindle whorls, loom weights, fishing equipment, and wooden household tools. Personal names scratched onto the handles of knives. Property marks cut into the beams of farmhouses. Short messages that read more like notes than formal inscriptions, the kind of thing a literate person dashes off without ceremony. The evidence suggests a society in which runic literacy, while not universal, was considerably more widespread than basic literacy in most contemporary medieval cultures. Learning to carve a few runes — one's own name, a protective formula, a simple message — was within the reach of many, not just specialists.

That said, there was clearly a tier of more accomplished practice. The carving of elaborate memorial runestones, or the inscription of complex magical formulas with correct phonetic precision, required genuine expertise. Some runestones name their own carvers, and a handful of names appear repeatedly across many stones — individuals who worked professionally, whose distinctive styles can be traced across a region. One carver active in eleventh-century Sweden, known from his signatures as Öpir, is credited with more than fifty runestones. His hand is recognizable across decades of work, suggesting a long career and a substantial local reputation. He was, in the fullest sense, an artist.

The picture of who carved runes is complicated further by the evidence for female practitioners. Several runic inscriptions name women as the carvers or commissioners of stones — not a curiosity but a pattern consistent enough to suggest that runic knowledge was not exclusively male territory. Some of the most elaborate memorial stones were raised by women for their husbands or sons, and the formulas used show a familiarity with the conventions of runic epigraphy that goes beyond simply hiring someone else for the task. In a society where inheritance, property rights, and public memory were all deeply tied to family networks, the ability to command and perhaps practice runic inscription would have been a meaningful form of social power.

The Uses of Runes

The range of purposes for which runes were used in Viking Age life resists reduction to any single category. At one end of the spectrum, the purely practical: property ownership, commercial transactions, the marking of personal possessions. Runes on a comb or a pair of shoes served much the same function as a name written in the front cover of a book — they identified what belonged to whom. At the other end, the explicitly sacred: protective inscriptions on weapons intended to give them power in battle, or formulas carved onto small amulets meant to be worn against the body.

Between these poles was the whole texture of ordinary life. Runestones erected in memory of the dead are the most numerous surviving monuments of the Viking Age — Sweden alone has more than three thousand — and they range from simple name-and-epitaph stones to elaborate narrative inscriptions that record journeys, battles, and lineages. Many were positioned along roads or at fords, where travelers would pass them regularly, so that the memory of the dead remained part of the living landscape. The stones were often painted in bright colors when first erected, their carved letters filled with red or black pigment so they could be read from a distance. Time and weather have stripped that color away, but the original intention was something vivid and public, a statement addressed to everyone who passed.

The intersection of the practical and the sacred could be very close. A sword was a practical object, but a sword with a protective rune carved into its blade was understood to carry something more than metal. The inscription did not merely decorate; it was believed to act. Runic formulas on weapons and armor, on the lintels of houses, on the prows of ships — these were understood as functional magic, calling on forces in the world to protect what mattered. The boundary between what we would call craft and what we would call religion was, for the people who used runes, far less distinct than it is for us.

The Coming of Christianity

The Christianization of Scandinavia was not an event but a process, unfolding over roughly two centuries and proceeding unevenly across different regions. Denmark converted earliest, in the mid-tenth century, when Harald Bluetooth — the king commemorated on the great Jelling Stones — officially adopted Christianity and raised a runestone announcing his accomplishment, in runes. Norway followed in stages across the late tenth and early eleventh centuries. Sweden held out the longest, with the last pagan strongholds converted only around 1100.

What is striking about this process, from the perspective of runic history, is how little disruption it initially caused to runic practice. The Jelling Stones themselves are the clearest evidence: a Christian king, celebrating his conversion, chose runes as the medium for his announcement. The two traditions coexisted, borrowed from each other, and ran in parallel for generations. Runestones from the eleventh century frequently incorporate Christian prayers and imagery alongside the traditional memorial formulas, the cross appearing next to the serpent-and-interlace patterns that had been decorating stones for decades.

Some of these hybrid stones are among the most visually striking objects the Viking Age produced. The great Jelling Stone raised by Harald Bluetooth around 965 CE carries an image of Christ rendered in the knotwork style of Norse art — the figure entangled in the same interlace that would have decorated a pagan monument — and is framed by a Younger Futhark inscription declaring that Harald "made the Danes Christian." The stone is a compressed history of a cultural transition: a new religion announced in the language and the script of the old one, wearing its formal conventions like a borrowed coat.

What changed more slowly was the context in which writing was taught and transmitted. As churches were built and monasteries established, Latin literacy became increasingly central to administrative and religious life. Scribal culture — the culture of parchment and ink, of trained copyists working in dedicated scriptoria — was a church institution, and it operated entirely in Latin. The knowledge required to carve runes was passed on informally, from individual to individual, outside any institutional structure. As Latin literacy became more valuable for navigating the emerging institutions of medieval Scandinavian society, runic literacy became, by degrees, less so.

The decline was not sharp. As the Bryggen inscriptions remind us, ordinary people were still writing in runes in Bergen well into the fourteenth century, long after the formal conversion. In remote communities, the practice persisted even longer. But the center of gravity had shifted. Runes moved from the mainstream to the margins, from the public road to the private transaction, and eventually — in all but the most isolated communities — into memory.

What the Runes Carry

There is something in the Viking relationship with the runes that resists the categories we tend to impose on the past. The runes were a writing system, yes, but also a symbolic vocabulary, a spiritual technology, a craft tradition, and a living connection to the mythology that structured the Norse world. They were used to record the mundane and to reach toward the divine, often in the same gesture.

Understanding this is, in some ways, the work of the rest of this book. The history covered in these first three chapters gives the runes their context — shows where they came from, how they developed, and in what kind of world they were most fully alive. But the deeper question of what the runes actually mean, and why they continue to speak to people today, requires going further back than history can reach, into the myths and cosmological stories that gave the symbols their original power.

That is where we are going next.

The Norse Cosmos: Gods and the Nine Worlds

E very culture builds a picture of the universe — a map of what exists, how it is organized, and where human life sits within it. For the Norse, that picture was unusually vivid. It was also unusually interconnected: the gods were not remote figures dispensing judgment from a distance but active presences in a shared world, subject to fate, capable of loss, and bound to a story that had both a beginning and an end. Understanding this cosmology is not background preparation for studying the runes. It is, in a real sense, part of studying them. The runes grew from this world, carried its logic in their names, and were believed to draw their power from its deepest structures.

The Sources

Almost everything we know about Norse mythology comes from two collections of texts, both written down in Iceland in the thirteenth century — well after the Viking Age had ended and Christianity had become the established religion of the Norse world. This is not a small complication. The people who wrote these texts were Christians, working at some distance from the living tradition they were recording, and the material they preserved had already passed through centuries of oral transmission. What survives is vivid and substantial, but it is not a clean window onto pre-Christian belief. It is more like a very good photograph of a landscape seen through imperfect glass.

The Poetic Edda is a collection of anonymous poems, gathered in a manuscript known as the Codex Regius, probably compiled around 1270. The poems themselves are older — some scholars date certain of them to the Viking Age — and they cover an enormous range: creation myths, heroic legends, wisdom literature, and the prophecy of the world's end. They were composed to be performed, and they carry in their compressed, allusive style the weight of an audience that already knew the stories. The poem that matters most for our purposes is the *Hávamál*, the "Words of the High One" — a long, composite text spoken in Odin's voice that includes, among much else, the account of how he won the runes.

The Prose Edda was written around 1220 by the Icelandic chieftain, poet, and historian Snorri Sturluson. Where the Poetic Edda is spare and assumes deep familiarity, Snorri explains. He retells the myths in narrative prose, glosses their meanings, and frames the whole within a framing device designed to make the old gods palatable to Christian readers. Snorri is indispensable — much of what we know about Norse mythology would be lost without him — but he is also a mediator, and his interests shaped what he chose to record and how he chose to present it.

The Tree at the Center

Norse cosmology organizes the universe around a single enormous axis: Yggdrasil, the World Tree. An ash of unimaginable size, Yggdrasil spans all of existence, its branches reaching into the heavens and its three roots extending down to three separate wells, each one a source of a different kind of knowledge or power. Around and within its structure are arrayed nine worlds, home to every category of being — gods, humans, giants, elves, dwarves, and the dead.

The tree is not merely a geographic convenience. It is a living structure through which the fate of everything flows. Beneath one of its roots lies the Well of Urðr, tended by the Norns, the three figures who shape the destiny of gods and mortals alike. Beneath another lies Mímisbrunnr, the Well of Mímir, source of wisdom so powerful that Odin sacrificed one of his eyes to drink from it. The tree itself is constantly under threat — gnawed by the dragon Níðhöggr at its roots, browsed by stags among its branches — and its health is identified with the health of the cosmos. When Yggdrasil shudders, the world trembles with it.

The three roots of Yggdrasil point in three different directions — toward Asgard, toward Jotunheim, toward the realm of the dead — and each draws nourishment from its own source. This structure is not decorative. The Norse understood the cosmos as something that required active maintenance, that could degrade and would degrade without the continuous labor of those who tended it: the Norns pouring water and white clay over the roots each day, the gods defending the boundaries between worlds, Odin gathering knowledge against the day he knows is coming. The universe in Norse thought is not stable by nature. It is held in place by ongoing effort, and the runes are part of that effort — tools for working with the forces that the tree embodies, not merely symbols describing them.

The Nine Worlds

The nine worlds of Norse cosmology each house a distinct order of being, and their relationships — sometimes cooperative, more often tense — drive much of the mythology. At the center of the human story is Midgard, the middle world, home of mortals, connected to the realm of the gods by Bifrost, the rainbow bridge. Above it, in the most elevated of the worlds, is Asgard, where the Aesir gods rule from their great hall and Odin presides over Valhalla, the hall of warriors slain in battle.

The other worlds range from the luminous to the extreme. Alfheim is the realm of the light elves, beings associated with fertility and creativity; Vanaheim is the home of the Vanir, the second family of gods, whose concerns are peace, fertility, and the cycles of nature. Jotunheim, the realm of the giants, sits in a state of permanent antagonism with Asgard — the jötnar are the gods' oldest adversaries, and also, in complicated ways, their kin. Svartalfheim is the underground realm of the dwarves, master craftspeople whose forges produced the most powerful objects in the cosmos: Odin's spear Gungnir, Thor's hammer Mjölnir, the ship Skiðblaðnir that folds to fit in a pocket. At the two primordial extremes are Muspelheim, the world of fire, presided over by the fire giant Surtr, and Niflheim, the world of ice and mist, the oldest of all the realms. Between them, in the myths of creation, the interaction of heat and cold generated the first life. And at the boundary of everything lies Helheim, the realm of the dead who died of illness or old age, ruled by Hel, daughter of Loki — a quiet world, neither punishment nor reward, simply the destination of those whose fate was not to die in battle.

The nine worlds and the three *aettir* of the Elder Futhark are not in explicit correspondence in the Norse sources — the connection is structural rather than stated. But it is worth holding in mind that the Elder Futhark's three groups of eight runes mirror the tree's own tripartite organization: three roots, three wells, three orders of time. The first *aett*, Freyr's, deals with the material world and the forces of generation — the level of Midgard and the living earth. The second, Heimdall's, deals with disruption, fate, and the forces that cannot be controlled — the level at which the Norns operate. The third, Tyr's, deals with order, sacrifice, and collective legacy — the level of the gods, whose decisions shape the cosmos. The runes map the tree's structure in compressed form.

The Norns

Of all the figures in Norse mythology, the three Norns hold a particular importance for anyone studying the runes. They are Urðr, Verðandi, and Skuld — names that carry within them the grammar of time, pointing toward what has been, what is becoming, and what is to come. They live at the foot of Yggdrasil beside the Well of Urðr, and each day they draw water from the well and mix it with the white clay of the shore, pouring it over the tree's roots to sustain it.

Their primary work is fate. They carve runes into the trunk of Yggdrasil to inscribe the destinies of gods and mortals — not predictions but determinations, the shaping of what will be. Every life, divine or human, unfolds according to what the Norns have written. Even Odin, the most powerful of the gods, operates within the structure they have laid down. He knows, for instance, that Ragnarök is coming, that he will be swallowed by the wolf Fenrir in the final battle, and that this knowledge changes nothing. He prepares anyway. He gathers the slain warriors of Valhalla. He acquires knowledge wherever he can find it. But the Norns' carving stands.

The Norse concept most closely tied to the Norns' work is ørlög — a word composed of ór (out of, from the beginning) and lög (law, layers). It refers to the primal law laid down at the origin of things, the accumulated weight of all that has been done and cannot be undone, the substrate of fate on which the present moment rests. Ørlög is not destiny in the sense of a fixed future; it is more like the total of everything that has already happened, exerting its pressure on what can now occur. The Norns weave with it, and the runes are its alphabet — each symbol a condensed law of the world, a principle that has been true from the beginning and will be true until the end.

This connection between the Norns and runic inscription is not incidental. When we encounter runes later in this book — in divination, in magical practice, in the daily work of self-reflection — part of what we are working within is this idea: that carved symbols can reach something real, can make contact with the forces that shape existence. The Norns are the first and greatest rune-carvers, and the tradition flows from them.

The Gods

The Aesir are the dominant family of Norse gods, and Odin is their head — a figure so complex that no single description does him justice. He is the god of war, but his interest in battle is less about violence than about what violence reveals: fate, courage, the limits of mortal endurance. He is the god of poetry, having won the mead of poetry through cunning and transformative shapeshifting. He is the god of wisdom, which he has pursued at extraordinary personal cost — one eye given to Mímir's well, nine days of self-inflicted torment on Yggdrasil to win the runes. He moves through the human world in disguise, a wanderer in a wide-brimmed hat, gathering knowledge and testing people. He is generous and he is treacherous. He is, of all the Norse gods, the most difficult to trust and the most interesting to follow.

Frigg, his wife, is the goddess of marriage, motherhood, and foresight. She knows the fate of all things but characteristically does not speak of what she knows — a silence that carries its own kind of power, and that distinguishes her prophetic gift from Odin's restless pursuit of knowledge. Her most famous moment in the mythology is her attempt to protect her son Baldr from the death she has foreseen, traveling through all the worlds to extract promises of non-harm from every substance and creature in existence. She fails because she overlooks mistletoe, judging it too young and harmless to need an oath. That oversight is precisely what Loki exploits.

Baldr, Odin and Frigg's son, is the god of light and purity, and his death is the mythology's central tragedy. Guided by Loki, the blind god Höðr throws a dart of mistletoe that kills Baldr instantly. The gods' attempts to retrieve him from Helheim fail by the narrowest of margins — one giantess refuses to weep for him, and the condition of his return requires universal mourning. Baldr remains in Helheim until after Ragnarök, when he returns to a remade world. His story is, among other things, a story about what cannot be protected, and about how loss is woven into the structure of existence.

Thor, Odin's son, is the defender of Asgard and Midgard against the jötnar who would overwhelm both. Armed with Mjölnir, he is direct where Odin is subtle, loyal where Loki is opportunistic, physical where Frigg is withdrawn. He is also, in the mythology, genuinely beloved — the god most closely identified with the protection of ordinary people, whose name was invoked for blessing at weddings and births. Thursday carries his name.

Loki occupies a position in Norse mythology that resists easy summary. He is of giant descent but lives among the Aesir, a shapeshifter and a catalyst, responsible for both the gods' greatest treasures and their worst disasters. He engineers the death of Baldr. He is eventually bound beneath the earth, his wife Sigyn holding a bowl over him to catch the venom dripping from a serpent above — her occasional need to empty the bowl producing the earthquakes the Norse understood as his writhing. He will break free at Ragnarök, where he will fight against the gods he once called family.

Freyja, of the Vanir, is the goddess of love, fertility, war, and magic — a combination that feels paradoxical until you understand how the Norse conceived of power. She is the foremost practitioner of seiðr, the form of shamanic magic that allows its user to perceive and alter the threads of fate, and it was from her that Odin learned it. She receives half of those slain in battle, filling her hall Fólkvangr as Odin fills Valhalla. Her twin brother Freyr governs the fertility of the land, the abundance of harvests, and the peace between peoples. He too sacrifices something irreplaceable — his sword, surrendered for love — and dies at Ragnarök without it.

Ragnarök

Norse cosmology does not end in stability. It ends in catastrophe: Ragnarök, the doom of the gods, a final battle in which most of the major divine figures are killed, the World Tree shudders, and the earth sinks into the sea. Fenrir swallows Odin. Thor kills the Midgard Serpent and dies from its venom nine steps later. The sun goes dark.

And then the world is remade. From the waters, a new earth rises, green and fertile. The surviving gods return. Baldr comes back from Helheim. Two humans, sheltered in the wood of Hoddmímis holt, emerge to repopulate Midgard. The cycle begins again.

The Norse understood existence as moving through cycles of formation, fullness, destruction, and renewal — not as a linear story with a single ending. The runes exist within this framework. They carry the energies of a cosmos that is always in process, always at some point in its cycle, always containing within it the seeds of what comes next. When you draw a rune, you are reaching into that cycle, asking a particular force to make itself visible at a particular moment. The rune that comes up is not random. It is, in the Norse understanding, the one whose season it currently is — the energy that *ørlög* has made available, rising to the surface of the present moment like water drawn from a very old well.

The Allfather's Sacrifice: How the Runes Were Born

B egin with the word itself. *Rune* descends from the Proto-Germanic *rūnō*, a word that carried, before it ever meant a letter, a cluster of meanings centered on secrecy and whispered speech: a secret, a mystery, something murmured between those who share a knowledge that others do not. In Old Irish, the related word *rún* means a secret or a close confidence. In Welsh, *rhin* carries a similar sense. The word spread across the Germanic languages with this weight already inside it — so that when the runic alphabet took the name, it was not simply being called a script. It was being called a system of secrets.

This etymology is the first clue to what the runes were understood to be. They were not a neutral technology for recording information. They were access points to something hidden in the structure of the world, symbols that, correctly understood and correctly used, could reach forces that lay beyond ordinary human perception. The question of how that access became available — how the runes came to exist at all — is answered by what is arguably the most important story in Norse mythology.

The Hávamál

The *Hávamál*, or "Words of the High One," is one of the longest and most complex poems in the Poetic Edda. It is spoken throughout in Odin's voice, and it is composite in character — an anthology of wisdom literature, practical advice, reflections on fate and friendship, and mythological narrative, assembled from material of varying age and provenance. Near its center sits a passage known to scholars as the *Rúnatal*, the "Enumeration of Runes," in which Odin describes in compressed, allusive language how he won the runes and what they gave him.

The poem is written in a style that assumes familiarity. It does not explain itself. It presents what happened with the spare directness of something that the audience was expected to already know, requiring the listener to bring their own understanding to the images. For a modern reader, this creates a peculiar experience: the poem feels simultaneously ancient and immediate, like a text that is not quite willing to be a text, that still carries within its written form the memory of being spoken aloud in a room where everyone leaned forward.

Nine Days on the Tree

The story behind the *Rúnatal* is this.

Before humans existed, before the present order of the worlds had fully settled, the runes lay at the bottom of the Well of Urðr — embedded in the same deep source from which the Norns drew the water they poured over Yggdrasil's roots each day. The runes were not invented. They were discovered, or rather revealed, like laws of physics that exist before anyone formulates them. The Norns knew them, and used them, carving their determinations into the bark of the World Tree. But the runes had not passed into general knowledge. They were, in the fullest sense of the word, secret.

Odin, watching the Norns work, recognized what was moving in their hands. This was knowledge of a kind he did not possess, and the fact that he did not possess it was insupportable to him. Odin's defining quality is not strength or courage or even wisdom in the ordinary sense. It is the absolute refusal to accept the boundaries of what he knows. He has already, by the time of this story, sacrificed one eye to drink from Mímir's well and gain the wisdom held there. That cost did not diminish his hunger. If anything, it sharpened it.

The runes, however, could not be taken or bargained for. They had to be earned. The condition of receiving them was proof of worthiness, and the only proof of worthiness the runes would accept was sacrifice — genuine, irreversible, freely chosen suffering. Odin understood this. He took his own spear, Gungnir, and wounded himself with it. Then he hung himself from a branch of Yggdrasil, head downward over the void, suspended between the world of the living and the depths of the well below.

He hung there for nine days and nine nights. He refused food and water. He refused the help that other gods moved to offer him, turning them back with a word. He was alone with what he had chosen, suspended between states, neither fully alive nor dead, holding himself in the threshold between knowing and not knowing. The nine is deliberate — nine is the number of the worlds, the number of Yggdrasil's branches, the number that appears repeatedly in Norse cosmology at moments of transformation and completion. This was not duration chosen for comfort. It was duration chosen for meaning.

On the ninth night, Odin looked down into the darkness of the well and the runes looked back. They rose toward him, and in that moment of mutual recognition, they passed into him — all their meanings, their sounds, their visual forms, the relationships between them, the ways they could be combined and invoked. The *Hávamál* describes his response with an image of sudden growth: he became wise, he thrived, he was led from word to word and from work to work, each understanding opening onto the next. The sacrifice had been completed. Its cost had been paid. And what was given in return was not a tool but a transformation.

A God Offered to a God

The line from the *Hávamál* that most exercised Norse scholars and theologians is the poem's description of the sacrifice as an offering "from myself to myself" — Odin giving Odin to Odin. The grammatical strangeness is not accidental. It points to something that the poem is working hard to say: that this sacrifice did not flow in the direction sacrifices usually flow, from the lesser toward the greater, from the mortal supplicant toward the divine power being petitioned. Here the god and the sacrifice and the recipient of the sacrifice are a single identity. There is no transaction between parties. There is only one party, going through a transformation that requires passing through something like death to reach something like rebirth.

This has led some scholars to read the Odin myth as a kind of shamanic initiation narrative, structurally similar to the death-and-return experiences described in shamanic traditions across many cultures — the novice who undergoes a symbolic death, often involving hanging or suspension, and returns with powers unavailable to those who have not made the crossing. Whether or not the Norse narrative drew on such traditions, the structural logic is the same: certain kinds of knowledge cannot be acquired through ordinary learning. They require a transformation in the person do-ing the learning. They require the willingness to lose something that cannot be recovered.

What Odin lost on the tree is not entirely clear from the sources. Part of it is legible — the nine days of pain and deprivation, the wound, the isolation. But the poem implies something deeper: that the Odin who descended from Yggdrasil was not quite the same as the one who had climbed it. Something had been shed. Something had been left behind in the purgatory between the living and the dead. This is the price of the runes, embedded in the mythology that created them: they came at a cost that could not be fully described, only borne.

The Word as Force

To understand why the runes were worth that cost, it helps to understand how the pre-Christian Germanic world thought about language.

In modern linguistics, the relationship between a word and the thing it names is generally understood as arbitrary. The English word "fire" and the Norse word *eldr* and the Latin word *ignis* all refer to the same phenomenon, with no intrinsic connection between the sound of the word and the nature of the thing. We invented the labels, and we could have invented different ones. Language, in this view, is a code — useful and powerful, but fundamentally a human convention rather than a property of the world itself.

The Germanic tradition held a different understanding. Before the arrival of Christianity, across the Norse and Germanic world, the spoken word was understood to be constitutive rather than merely descriptive. To name something was not to label it from the outside but to call it into presence — to make contact with the force or principle the name contained. Speaking a word out loud committed something irreversible to the world. An oath spoken was an oath bound into reality by the act of speaking. A curse uttered could not simply be taken back. A name correctly invoked reached whatever it named.

This was not merely philosophical. It was built into the legal and social fabric of Norse life in ways that had practical consequences. The oath sworn at the *thing* — the public assembly — was not simply a promise that could be repudiated if inconvenient. It was a speech act that changed the speaker's standing in the world, that called the gods as witnesses, that bound fate in ways which transgression would unravel at severe cost. The Eddas are full of moments when a character's words, spoken carelessly or in ignorance of their full weight, produce consequences that cannot be undone. Loki's casual promise to Þjazi. Frigg's oversight in not extracting an oath from mistletoe. The words that could not be recalled, the names that had been spoken into the world and now had to be lived with. The Norse understanding of language was not abstract. It was a lived experience of consequence.

This is not simply superstition or metaphor. It is a coherent theory of language that certain contemporary thinkers have moved back toward from unexpected directions. The twentieth-century philosopher Martin Heidegger, working largely outside any awareness of Norse tradition, developed an account of language that resonates with what the rune-carvers appear to have understood. For Heidegger, language is not a tool that humans use to describe a world that exists independently of it. Language is the medium in which the world appears to us at all. We do not first perceive and then name; we perceive through naming. The words available to us shape the reality we are able to inhabit. In this sense, language is not descriptive but world-making.

The Germanic understanding of runic power follows exactly this logic. Each rune is not a symbol for a concept but a participation in the force the concept names. Fehu does not mean "cattle and wealth"; Fehu is the energy of wealth moving through the world, rendered visible and audible in a form that can be worked with.

Uruz does not mean "wild ox and strength"; Uruz is the force of untamed vitality itself, given a shape that a human hand can carve and a human voice can chant.

Phonosemantics and the Runic Name

The study of phonosemantics — the investigation of whether sound and meaning are intrinsically connected, rather than arbitrarily paired — remains contested in modern linguistics, but it has accumulated enough evidence to be taken seriously. Across unrelated languages, certain sound patterns cluster around similar meanings with a frequency that is difficult to explain as coincidence alone. The Germanic runic tradition was built on an assumption of exactly this kind of intrinsic connection, extended and deepened to include the visual form of each letter alongside its sound.

Each rune in the Elder Futhark has a name, a sound, and a shape, and the Norse understanding was that all three pointed toward the same underlying reality. Tiwaz, the rune associated with the god Tyr, is shaped like a spear or an upward-pointing arrow. Tyr was the god of law and justice and single combat — the one who sacrificed his hand to bind the wolf Fenrir, accepting permanent injury in exchange for the safety of the other gods. The rune that carries his name points upward, toward the sky in which he dwelt, and the shape encodes the qualities he represents: directness, aim, the will that holds its course. The name, the sound, the shape, and the meaning are not four different things. They are four aspects of a single thing, a knot of significance tying a letter to a cosmic principle.

Here the concept of ørlög — introduced in the previous chapter — becomes relevant again. The Norse word means, roughly, the primal law laid down at the origin of things: the total weight of everything that has been done and cannot be undone, pressing on the present moment. If ørlög is the substrate of fate, the rune names are its vocabulary. Each name is not a label attached after the fact to a force that existed independently. Each name is a compression of the force itself — the sound through which *fehu's* energy of flowing wealth has always expressed itself, the shape through which *uruz's* vitality has always been visible, reaching back before language was written down and before the alphabet that carries them was assembled. The runes emerged from the Well of Urðr because the well contains everything that has always been true. They were there before Odin hung to receive them.

This is what Odin brought back from the nine days on Yggdrasil: not a set of letters, but a set of knots. Twenty-four compressed relationships between sound, image, and the deep forces that organize the world. The runes he won were tools for reaching those forces — for invoking them, meditating on them, drawing them into specific situations through carving or chanting or contemplation. The mythology of the sacrifice is, in this reading, the founding story of an entire practice: the idea that the symbols available to us are not arbitrary marks but living connections to something real.

What This Means for the Reader

It would be easy to hold this at a distance as a piece of cultural history — interesting, evocative, but belonging to a world that is no longer ours. That distance is available if you want it. But many people who work with the runes today find that holding the mythology closer, rather than further away, changes the quality of the practice.

When you draw a rune in the morning and sit with its name and its shape, you are doing something that carries the imprint of Odin's descent — not because you share his cosmology in every detail, but because the act is structurally the same: a deliberate entry into the threshold between what you know and what you do not, a willingness to receive something that cannot be predicted or controlled, a trust that the symbol will speak if you are quiet enough to hear it. The sacrifice at the center of the founding myth is a model for what every runic practice asks of the person who undertakes it. You have to be willing to hang there a while, in the space between the question and the answer, without reaching for certainty.

That willingness is what the runes were born from. It is also what they reward.

The Twenty-Four – The Elder Futhark

T he twenty-four runes of the Elder Futhark are not a list. They are a sequence, and the sequence matters. Each rune follows from the one before it and prepares the ground for the one after, in the same way that a year moves through seasons, or a life moves through its stages. The Norse organized this sequence into three groups of eight – the three *aettir*, or clans – each one presided over by a deity whose nature colors the runes within it.

The first *aett* belongs to Freyr, god of fertility, abundance, and the generative forces of the natural world. Its eight runes deal with the foundations of existence: the material world, the body, physical vitality, the energy required to begin things, the joy of being alive. They are not simple runes – none of them are – but they are grounded, concerned with what is present and immediate.

The second *aett* belongs to Heimdall, the watchman of the gods, who stands at the boundary between the worlds. His eight runes deal with disruption, transformation, and the forces that cannot be controlled or anticipated. They are the runes of the middle of the journey, when the initial energy of departure has been spent and the destination is not yet in sight.

The third *aett* belongs to Tyr, the god of law, justice, and ordered sacrifice. His eight runes deal with the principles that hold things together: community, legacy, the relationship between the individual and the larger patterns of which they are a part. They are the runes of maturity and integration.

Together the three *aettir* tell a story about what it means to move through a life: to begin with energy and desire, to be broken open by what cannot be foreseen, and to arrive — if you are paying attention — at something larger than what you started with. Each rune in each *aett* is a chapter of that story. What follows is a close reading of all twenty-four.

A note on how these descriptions are structured. For each rune you will find three movements: first, the symbol — its name, its sound, its visual form, and the etymological root that connects the letter to its core meaning. Second, the meaning — what the rune says when it appears upright in a reading, and what it says when it appears reversed or *merkstave*. These are not opposites but complements, two aspects of the same energy seen from different angles. Third, the practice — how this rune tends to show up in daily life, what it invites you to notice, and how you might work with it directly.

The runes are not a fixed code. They are a vocabulary, and like any vocabulary, they grow richer the longer you work with them. What is offered here is a starting point, not a destination.

The First Aett: Freyr's Aett

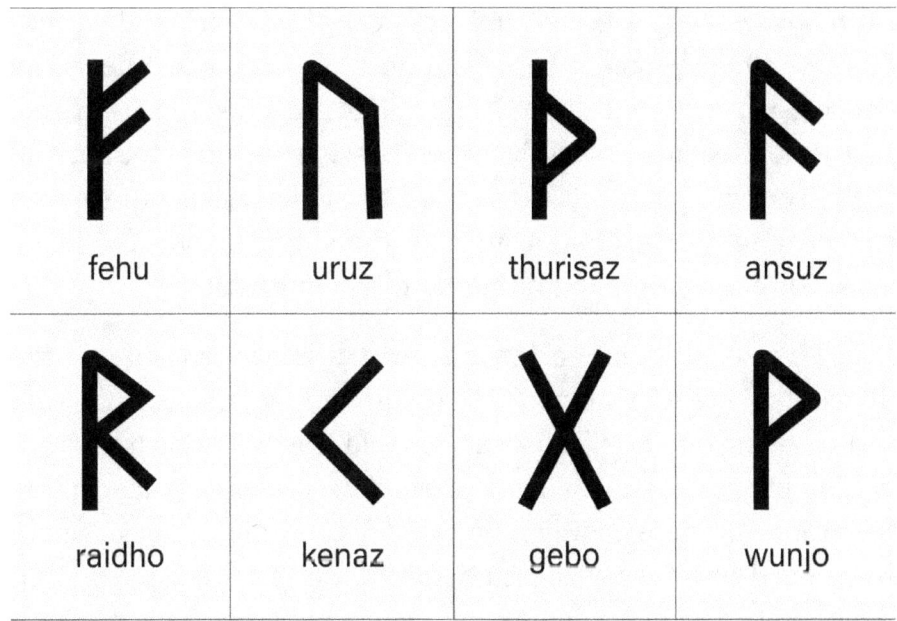

fehu	uruz	thurisaz	ansuz
raidho	kenaz	gebo	wunjo

Fehu (*fey-hoo*)

The first rune of the Elder Futhark takes its name from the Pro-to-Germanic word for cattle. In the Norse world, cattle were the primary measure of wealth — not coins, not land in the abstract, but animals: living, mobile, productive. A person's herd was their fortune, visible to everyone and capable of growth. Fehu, then, begins where everything begins, with the most immediate and tangible form of what we need and desire. Its shape — a vertical staff with two diagonal branches angling upward to the right — suggests something reaching, extending outward, sending energy forward into the world.

When Fehu appears in a reading, it speaks to the movement of material and energetic resources. Wealth coming in, or already present and available to be put to use. But Fehu's understanding of wealth is broader than the purely financial. It covers any form of abundance — creative energy, social capital, physical vitality, luck in the sense of a favorable alignment between effort and outcome. The rune's deepest concern is with circulation: wealth that flows, that is shared, that generates more of itself through use. Fehu is not the rune of the miser who hoards. It is the rune of the generous farmer who reinvests in the herd, knowing that the abundance of the living grows through movement rather than accumulation.

In its reversed position, Fehu points toward stagnation or loss in the material sphere — money worries, drained energy, a sense that what you are doing is not yielding what it should. The invitation here is not despair but reassessment. Fehu reversed asks where the circulation has stopped, where energy is being held rather than moved, where plans need to be reconsidered before more resources are poured into them. It can also point to a misalignment between what you are pursuing and what actually matters to you — chasing the wrong kind of wealth, measured by someone else's standard.

Working with Fehu means developing a conscious relationship with whatever you consider prosperity. This is rarely as simple as it sounds. Many of us carry inherited ideas about money, abundance, and worthiness that operate below the level of deliberate thought. Drawing Fehu in a daily practice is an invitation to examine those ideas — to ask what wealth means to you, not in the abstract, but in the specific choices you made this week. What did you give? What did you receive? What did you hold back, and why?

Uruz (oo-*rooze*)

The second rune names an animal that no longer exists. The aurochs — *ur* in Proto-Germanic — was the wild ancestor of domestic cattle, a massive and formidable creature that stood nearly six feet at the shoulder and ranged across the forests of Europe until its extinction in the seventeenth century. Where Fehu's cattle were tamed and productive, Uruz's aurochs was wild, dangerous, and ungovernable. The contrast between the two runes is immediate and deliberate: after the rune of cultivated wealth comes the rune of raw, untamed force.

Uruz in a reading speaks to the body's strength, to stamina and health, to the kind of deep vitality that enables sustained effort over time. It is the energy underneath the energy — not the immediate enthusiasm of beginning but the physical and psychological reserves that determine whether you can carry something to completion. When Uruz appears, it often marks a period of renewed vigor, or points to resources of endurance that are available and not yet fully drawn on. It can also carry a cautionary dimension: power this undirected can overwhelm as easily as it can propel, and the rune sometimes appears as a reminder to channel rather than simply release.

Reversed, Uruz speaks to depletion — the body exhausted, the reserves run low, a period of diminished capacity. This is not failure; it is physics. Energy spent faster than it is replenished eventually runs out. Uruz reversed invites rest and recovery, a reconsideration of what is being demanded of your body and your psyche, a reassessment of whether the pace you are keeping is sustainable. It can also point to a missed opportunity — a moment when strength was available and not used, when hesitation or self-doubt kept you from acting on what you were capable of.

The deeper teaching of Uruz is about the relationship between wild force and conscious direction. The aurochs cannot be trained, but its descendants can — and the transition from Uruz to Fehu in the sequence maps exactly this movement, from raw capacity to cultivated resource. Working with Uruz means being honest about your physical and energetic condition: not the idealized version of yourself you present to the world, but the actual state of your body, your sleep, your appetite for the life you are living.

Thurisaz (*thoo-ree-sahz*)

The third rune sits at an uncomfortable angle to the two that precede it. After abundance and vitality comes Thurisaz — the rune of the thorn, the giant, the hammer. Its shape is sharp and asymmetrical: a vertical staff with a single triangular projection pointing to the right, like a thorn or the head of a weapon. The name connects to the Proto-Germanic Þurisaz, a word for giant or thurse, the beings who in Norse mythology represent chaos and the forces that oppose the ordered world of the gods.

Thurisaz is the first rune in the Elder Futhark that refuses easy comfort. It is associated with Thor's hammer Mjölnir, which is both a weapon and a tool of protection — capable of tremendous destruction when wielded against the enemies of order, but never something to handle carelessly. This duality is the rune's central lesson. The energy that can break down is the same energy that can defend. The force that causes harm, misdirected, is also the force that protects, correctly aimed. The question Thurisaz always asks is which direction the force is moving in.

In a reading, Thurisaz often marks a moment requiring confrontation — with an obstacle, with a person, with an aspect of yourself you have been avoiding. The rune does not enjoy indirect approaches. It pushes toward directness, toward naming what is actually happening rather than managing the situation from a careful distance. When it appears before a decision or action, it often counsels pause — not avoidance, but the deliberate stillness before a decisive move, the breath taken before speaking the difficult truth. Catharsis is part of its territory: the clearing that can only happen after something has been broken down.

Reversed, Thurisaz points to the shadow of this energy: aggression that serves no protective purpose, defensiveness that misreads a situation, a wound made carelessly that cannot be easily undone. It can indicate vulnerability — defenses lowered at the wrong moment, or a tendency to lash out when feeling threatened. The reversed rune asks whether the conflict it senses is real or manufactured, whether the force being deployed is proportionate, whether the battle being prepared for is actually necessary.

Working with Thurisaz means becoming more honest about how you handle discomfort and confrontation. Most of us default either to avoidance or escalation, and Thurisaz invites a third option: deliberate engagement, neither running from what is hard nor forcing a resolution before one is ready.

Ansuz (*ahn-sooze*)

The fourth rune takes its name from the Old Norse word for a deity of the Aesir — specifically, the divine principle associated with Odin, the god of wisdom, speech, and the breath of life. Its shape is similar to the modern letter F but with both horizontal branches angling downward, as if the energy moves not just forward but back, inward, through. Ansuz is the rune of communication in its deepest sense: not just the exchange of words but the whole architecture of meaning-making — the capacity to perceive, to interpret, to speak, to listen, to name.

The etymological connection to breath is important. In Norse understanding, breath was the carrier of the divine — the first gift that Odin, along with his brothers, gave to the first humans, Ask and Embla, was the breath that animated them. Ansuz governs all the phenomena that depend on this gift: language and song, learning and teaching, divination and prophecy, the pattern-recognition that allows a mind to find order in apparent chaos. When Ansuz appears, it often signals that communication — inward or outward — is the key to whatever situation is being examined. Messages in transit, insight on its way, a word that needs to be spoken or a listening that needs to happen.

The rune's connection to Odin also brings a warning built into its gift. Odin's communication is never wholly straightforward. He speaks in riddles, tests through disguise, teaches through the displacement of expectation. Ansuz in a reading can therefore point to misunderstanding as easily as clarity — to the need to examine whether you are hearing what is actually being said, or interpreting through the filter of what you expect or fear. It governs the capacity for deception as readily as for truth, and its appearance sometimes asks a direct question: are you being honest, with others or with yourself?

Reversed, Ansuz amplifies these shadow qualities — miscommunication, manipulation, the use of language to obscure rather than reveal. It can mark a period of mental static, when clear thought is difficult and the signals coming in from the outside world seem hard to interpret. The reversed rune often calls for silence and simplification: less input, more stillness, a return to the practice of listening before speaking.

Daily work with Ansuz attends to the quality of your internal monologue as much as your outer speech. The rune asks how you are speaking to yourself — whether the language you use to narrate your own life is accurate and generous, or distorted by habits of self-diminishment or self-inflation. The way you speak inwardly shapes, far more than most people realize, the world you are able to perceive.

Raidho *(rye-tho)*

The fifth rune names a journey. Its Proto-Germanic root *raidō* means a riding, a vehicle, the act of deliberate movement through space. Raidho's shape — a vertical line with a curved arm projecting to the upper right and a diagonal leg dropping to the lower right — suggests something in motion, a figure in mid-stride. The rune governs all forms of travel, literal and symbolic: the road trip and the spiritual passage, the move to a new city and the shift in perspective that comes from committing to a direction and following it through.

Raidho in a reading speaks to movement, rhythm, and the alignment between where you are and where you are going. It is a favorable sign for any undertaking that requires sustained effort over time — travel, of course, but also long projects, evolving relationships, periods of growth that unfold gradually rather than all at once. The rune carries a sense of rightness about a chosen direction, an internal compass pointing true north. When Raidho appears alongside questions about decisions or transitions, it often confirms that the movement being considered is the right one, while also reminding the querent that the journey itself is where the value lies, not only the destination.

The rune's concern with rhythm is worth dwelling on. Raidho does not just mean movement — it means measured, ordered movement, the kind that can be sustained. A rider in Norse culture was not simply someone who traveled but someone who understood the relationship between horse and terrain and pace, who knew when to push and when to rest, who read the ground ahead rather than only following the path behind. Raidho asks you to be this kind of traveler in your own life.

Reversed, Raidho signals disruption of movement — delays, detours, obstacles on a path that seemed clear. Plans going sideways. A journey taken in the wrong direction, or at the wrong time. The reversed rune can point to a situation where the external movement is proceeding but the internal compass is off — where you are going somewhere without actually having chosen where that somewhere is. It invites a check-in with your actual desires, beneath the momentum of habit or expectation.

The practice that Raidho most directly supports is the development of what might be called a personal navigation: the capacity to know, at any given moment, not just what you are doing but why you are doing it and whether it is taking you somewhere you genuinely want to go.

Kenaz (*kay-nahz*)

The sixth rune carries the image of a torch. Its name descends from the Proto-Germanic *kaunan*, a word for torch or beacon, the controlled fire that allows work to continue after dark and that marks, in the darkness, the location of something important. Kenaz is the rune of applied knowledge — not knowledge in the abstract but knowledge put to use, the skill in the craftsperson's hands, the understanding that has been tested against reality and proved. Its shape, a simple angle pointing to the right, looks like a flame viewed from the side, or the opening of something that was previously closed.

Kenaz in a reading speaks to creative energy, to learning, and to the specific quality of illumination that comes from understanding something that was previously obscure. This is not just intellectual light — it is the particular clarity that arrives when you have worked at something long enough that it begins to work back, when a skill you have been building starts to feel natural, when a situation you have been confused by suddenly becomes legible. The rune marks these moments of breakthrough and affirms that the path forward runs through engagement and practice rather than waiting for inspiration to arrive.

The ancestral dimension of Kenaz is significant. A torch passed down is a torch that carries the flame of those who carried it before — craftspeople transmitting their knowledge to apprentices, teachers to students, parents to children. Kenaz governs the living chain of transmitted understanding, and when it appears in a reading, it sometimes points to the importance of a teacher, a mentor, a tradition that deserves deeper engagement.

Reversed, Kenaz marks the failure or dimming of this light — creative stagnation, the feeling of being stuck in the dark without a clear direction, the loss of motivation or inspiration that can accompany a period of uncertainty. It can indicate the end of something: a project, a relationship, a phase of learning that has reached its natural limit. The reversed rune does not ask for forced enthusiasm. It asks for honest acknowledgment that the light has gone out in a particular direction, and that finding the next torch may require moving away from where you have been.

Working daily with Kenaz means paying attention to what genuinely lights you up — where your curiosity runs forward without being pushed, where learning feels like discovery rather than obligation. The rune has little patience for performed engagement. It points toward what actually calls to you, however inconvenient or unexpected that may be.

Gebo (*gay-bo*)

The seventh rune is shaped like an X — a perfect intersection, two lines crossing at equal angles, a form that is the same from every direction. Gebo means gift. Its name is cognate with the Old Norse *gjöf*, a word that carried in the Norse world a weight that the English word "gift" has mostly lost. In a culture built on reciprocal obligation, a gift was not a simple transaction but the creation of a bond — between giver and receiver, between host and guest, between a king and his retainers. To give was to bind. To receive was to incur a responsibility. The gift circulated, and the circulation was the relationship.

Gebo in a reading speaks to all forms of exchange, partnership, and reciprocity. Love relationships and professional partnerships, the exchange between a student and teacher, the bond between a person and a practice or a calling. It speaks to balance — not the mechanical equality of two identical things but the living equilibrium of a relationship where both parties give what they can and receive what they need. Gebo has no reversed position, which is notable. The energy of gift and exchange does not invert into an opposite; it distorts instead into imbalance — giving too much, receiving too little, or the reverse.

The question Gebo poses in its shadow reading is therefore not about absence but about proportion. Are you giving from genuine abundance, or from a compulsive need to be needed? Are you receiving with grace, or do you struggle to let generosity in? The rune asks whether the exchange at the center of the situation you are examining is actually balanced — whether the energy is flowing in both directions or has calcified into a one-sided pattern.

At its deepest level, Gebo points toward the most fundamental exchange in Norse cosmology: Odin giving himself to himself on Yggdrasil, the sacrifice where giver, gift, and recipient are one. This is the rune's highest expression — not the giving that seeks return, but the giving that is its own completion, the creative act offered without condition.

In daily practice, Gebo asks you to trace the exchanges in your life with some honesty: where you give, where you receive, where the flow is easy and where it has become stuck.

Wunjo (*woon-yo*)

The eighth and final rune of Freyr's Aett is a rune of joy — not the performative happiness of someone who has decided to be positive, but the deep, quiet gladness of a person whose life is in alignment with what they actually value. Wunjo's name comes from the Proto-Germanic *wunjō*, related to words for wish, desire, and the fulfillment of both. Its shape resembles a flag or pennant atop a staff: something raised up, visible, belonging to a particular clan or household, marking a place as inhabited and alive.

In Norse culture, the *wunjo* — the clan's banner — was a symbol of collective identity and belonging. Wunjo governs this dimension of experience: the sense of being among people with whom you share something real, of being part of something larger than yourself without losing yourself in it. The rune marks moments when effort and circumstance have aligned, when the work you have been doing begins to yield something that feels genuinely worthwhile, when relationships are nourishing rather than draining, when life has a quality of rightness that does not require explanation.

Wunjo in a reading is generally a welcome sight — a confirmation that things are moving in the right direction, that joy is available and not merely theoretical. For matters of relationship, it is a strong positive indicator. For matters of creativity or work, it suggests a period of productive flow. The rune is also associated with the law of attraction in a non-mystical sense: what we genuinely desire, as distinct from what we think we should desire, tends to draw its own fulfillment toward it. Wunjo points toward authentic desire rather than performed aspiration.

Reversed, Wunjo marks the presence of something blocking this alignment — discord, alienation, the feeling of being out of step with your own life. Anxiety, a sense of disconnection from people or purposes that should feel meaningful, the particular sadness of being in the right place for someone else's life rather than your own. The reversed rune often appears when external circumstances have become misaligned with internal reality, when the life being lived is being lived for appearances rather than genuine fulfillment.

The practice that Wunjo calls for is deceptively simple and genuinely difficult: to be honest about what actually brings you joy, as distinct from what you believe should bring you joy, what you have been told to want, what would look good from the outside. The rune's gift is clarity about this distinction. Its demand is the willingness to act on what you find.

Freyr's Aett closes here, at the place where the foundations of a life — material security, physical vitality, the capacity to act and communicate and move and learn and give and receive — meet the question of whether it is a life that actually satisfies. The eight runes together describe the complete ground floor of human experience. Everything that follows is built on them.ections.

The Second Aett: Heimdall's Aett

ᚺ	ᚾ	ᛁ	ᛃ
hagalaz	nauthiz	isa	jera
ᛇ	ᛈ	ᛉ	ᛊ
eihwaz	perthro	algiz	sowilo

Heimdall stands at the edge of everything. The watchman of Asgard, posted at the foot of the rainbow bridge Bifrost, he sees in all directions at once — his sight extending to the ends of the earth, his hearing so acute he can perceive the grass growing and the wool growing on the backs of sheep. He does not act; he watches. He does not intervene; he knows when intervention will be necessary. His role is the most exposed and in some ways the most thankless of all the gods: to stand at the boundary, awake while others sleep, alert to the approach of what cannot yet be seen.

The eight runes that bear his name carry his quality. Where Freyr's Aett moved through the sunlit world of desire and vitality and joy, Heimdall's Aett begins at the border — the place where the ordered life encounters what it cannot predict or control. These are the runes of disruption, of waiting, of the harvest earned by patience, of fate and mystery and the careful navigation of forces larger than any individual will. They are not comfortable runes, for the most part. They are true ones.

Hagalaz (haw-gaw-lahz)

Hail falls without warning. It does not discriminate between the deserving and the undeserving, the prepared and the unprepared. It destroys what is in its path — the crops near harvest, the animals in the field, the plans carefully laid — and it is over before any response is possible. Hagalaz, the ninth rune of the Elder Futhark and the first of Heimdall's Aett, takes its name from this phenomenon. Its shape in many runic traditions resembles a snowflake or a lattice — two diagonal lines crossing a vertical staff — a form that holds within it both the symmetry of a natural pattern and the sense of something falling from above.

Hagalaz is the rune of disruption that cannot be argued with. Not the disruption of poor planning or bad decisions — those have human causes and human remedies — but the disruption that arrives from outside the system of cause and effect you have been operating within. The illness that comes despite every precaution. The loss that arrives at the wrong time. The circumstance that was nobody's fault and cannot be fixed, only endured. Hagalaz does not carry a reversed meaning, which is consistent with its nature. Hail does not have a positive position. It falls.

What the rune offers in its falling is not comfort but a kind of clarity. Hagalaz marks the moment when the illusion of control is stripped away, and that stripping, painful as it is, can reveal something that was obscured by the normal maintenance of ordinary life. The Norse understood catastrophe as having an inherently revelatory function — not because suffering is good in itself, but because the encounter with what cannot be managed forces a reckoning with what actually matters. The hail that destroys the harvest also clears the field for the next planting.

In practice, Hagalaz tends to appear either at or just before moments of significant turbulence. Its presence in a reading asks for a particular quality of response: not the scrambling attempt to prevent what is already in motion, but the steadiness to hold your position while the storm passes. The rune marks a threshold. On the other side of what Hagalaz brings is almost always a changed landscape — and within that change, if you are paying attention, the seeds of something new.

Nauthiz (*now-theez*)

After the violence of hail comes the cold, insistent pressure of need. Nauthiz — the tenth rune, its name from the Proto-Germanic word for necessity or need — is the rune of constraint, of the conditions that cannot be avoided, of the moment when you come face to face with what is genuinely required as distinct from what you merely want. Its shape, a vertical staff crossed by a diagonal, looks like the friction fire-stick used by Norse people to start flame: two pieces of wood, one pressed against the other until heat is generated from resistance itself.

This image is Nauthiz in miniature. The rune does not work against resistance; it works through it. Necessity, in the Norse understanding, was not merely an obstacle but a force — the force that compels development in the way that no amount of comfort or ease can. It is precisely because the fire does not come without friction that the fire, when it comes, is real. Nauthiz asks you to understand what you actually need as distinct from what you have been pursuing, and to find in the gap between those two things the energy that drives genuine growth.

In a reading, Nauthiz often marks a period of limitation — resources constrained, options narrowed, the sense of being pressed on all sides. Its invitation in these moments is to examine the quality of what the constraint is revealing. Scarcity clarifies priorities. The person who cannot have everything must decide what they will have, and that decision, forced by necessity, tends to be more honest than the choices made from a position of abundance. Nauthiz asks: what do you actually need to survive and flourish? Not what you have been told to want, not what looks good from the outside — what is genuinely necessary for the life you are actually living?

Reversed, Nauthiz amplifies the shadow of constraint — the paralysis that comes from need unacknowledged, the anxiety of scarcity that has become a lens distorting all perception, the misdirection of energy into meeting needs that are not real needs at all. The reversed rune asks whether the limitations currently felt are actual or imagined, whether the desperation driving behavior is proportionate to the actual situation or is a pattern older than the current circumstances.

Working with Nauthiz means developing the discipline to distinguish need from desire consistently and honestly — a practice that sounds simple and is in fact one of the more demanding things a person can undertake.

Isa (ee-sah)

Ice stops everything. It does not destroy in the sudden violent way of hail; it arrests, suspends, holds in place what was moving. Isa, the eleventh rune, means ice, and its form is the simplest in the entire Elder Futhark: a single vertical line, unchanged, undivided, offering nothing to the eye beyond itself. It is the rune of pure stillness.

This simplicity is not emptiness. Ice holds within it the water it has become, and the water holds within it the potential of spring. Isa is a rune of suspension rather than conclusion — a pause in the movement of things that may feel like stagnation but is more accurately understood as gestation, the interval in which what is becoming next is taking shape out of sight. The Norse, living through winters that lasted for months, understood ice not only as a threat but as a season with its own logic: a time when the above-ground world was dormant, when the work of survival was different from the work of abundance, when patience was not a virtue to be cultivated but simply the only viable stance.

In a reading, Isa marks exactly this kind of pause — a period in which forward movement is genuinely not available, when pushing harder will not produce results and the appropriate response is to wait with as much equanimity as can be mustered. This is rarely what a querent wants to hear. The rune does not apologize for its message. It simply holds its ground, a single still line, and waits for the question to catch up to it.

Isa carries no reversed meaning. Ice is ice from every angle. What changes is your relationship to it. The rune's secondary teaching concerns the ego — the self-concept that, unchecked, can freeze into something rigid and brittle, mistaking its own boundaries for the boundaries of the world. Isa asks whether the stillness currently experienced is imposed from outside or generated from within, whether the ice is a season or a permanent condition, whether the patience the moment requires is being met with genuine acceptance or with the particular misery of forced waiting.

In daily practice, Isa is most useful as a check against unnecessary action — the rune that asks whether the impulse to move is genuine or simply the product of discomfort with stillness. Sitting quietly with Isa for a few minutes is one of the more instructive things a beginning rune practitioner can do.

Jera (*yair-ah*)

The twelfth rune turns the wheel. Jera means year — the full cycle, winter through winter, completion following completion — and its shape enacts what it names: two mirror-image forms rotating around a center point, each one implying the other, neither one stable without its counterpart. It is the rune of the harvest, but only in the sense that the harvest is inseparable from the planting, the tending, the long waiting, and the acceptance that the crop will come in its own time or not at all.

Jera follows Isa in the sequence with a particular appropriateness. After the frozen stillness of winter comes the return of movement, the thaw, the evidence that the patience required by the preceding rune was not wasted. Jera is the confirmation that cycles work — that effort sustained through difficult seasons accumulates, and that the long slow process of growth eventually reaches the moment when its results can be gathered. It is one of the most affirmative runes in the Elder Futhark, not because it promises ease, but because it embodies the bedrock principle that consistent, correctly aligned effort bears fruit.

The agricultural metaphor runs deep in Jera. The farmer who works this rune's wisdom does not plant in autumn and expect a harvest in a week. They prepare the soil, sow at the right time, tend through the growing season, and harvest when the crop is ready — not before, not after. Jera governs the alignment between timing and action, the understanding that the same effort applied at the wrong moment yields nothing, while the same effort at the right moment yields abundance. When Jera appears in a reading, it often asks about this alignment: are you working with the natural rhythm of the situation, or against it?

Jera carries no reversed meaning, which reflects its identification with the cycle itself rather than any particular point within it. The wheel always turns. What changes is only where you are in its rotation, and whether you are paying attention to where you are. In readings involving long-term projects, relationships that have developed slowly, or situations requiring more patience than the querent has so far been willing to extend, Jera is often a quiet reminder that the harvest comes for those who stay through the season.

The practice Jera most directly supports is the keeping of long records — the kind of journal or notebook that allows you to look back across months or years and see the growth that was invisible while it was happening.

Eihwaz (ay-wahz)

The thirteenth rune stands at the precise center of the Elder Futhark's twenty-four symbols, and what it names is the tree that stands at the center of the world. Eihwaz takes its name from the Proto-Germanic word for yew, a tree that is simultaneously one of the most toxic and one of the longest-lived plants in the Northern European landscape. A yew can survive for thousands of years. When its central trunk dies, new growth emerges from within the decay, and the tree continues — a living illustration of renewal generated not from health but from death. Ancient yews were planted in churchyards throughout Britain and Scandinavia not, as is sometimes assumed, because Christianity brought them there, but because they were there before Christianity arrived, already associated with the boundary between the living and the dead.

Eihwaz governs this boundary. It is the rune of the axis mundi, the vertical line connecting the worlds above and below, the spine of the cosmos through which the energies of the different realms flow. Its shape — a vertical line with two diagonal branches, one reaching up and one reaching down — enacts exactly this: a form that simultaneously points toward the heavens and the underworld, that holds both directions in a single continuous movement. The rune sits at the center of the sequence because it represents the turning point: the moment in the cycle when the direction shifts, when the outward movement of the first twelve runes gives way to the return of the second twelve.

In a reading, Eihwaz appears at moments of deep transition — particularly the kind that involves the death of something that has been central to your sense of who you are. Not all endings are Eihwaz endings; this rune marks the ones from which there is genuine transformation, the passages through which you emerge different rather than simply diminished. It asks for the willingness that the yew tree demonstrates: to let the old form decay without panic, trusting that what will grow from within the loss has its own integrity.

Reversed, Eihwaz points to a confusion or disorientation at the transitional threshold — the inability to let go of what is already ending, or the premature abandonment of something that still has life in it. The reversal often appears when fear of loss is masquerading as wisdom, when the appearance of moving forward is actually a flight from a necessary reckoning.

Eihwaz is also the rune most directly associated with the capacity to hold two apparently opposite truths simultaneously: that endings are real, and that they are not the end. This is not a comfortable rune to work with. It is a reliable one.

Perthro (pair-thro)

The fourteenth rune is the Elder Futhark's great enigma. Perthro's name is the one scholars have had the most difficulty reconstructing with confidence — the meaning of the Proto-Germanic root remains genuinely uncertain, which gives the rune, almost poetically, an identification with the very quality it embodies: the unknown, the hidden, the thing that cannot be pinned down. Its shape is most often described as a dice cup viewed from the side — an open vessel tilted on its axis, ready to receive or to release whatever falls from it.

Dice cups and lots were instruments of fate in the Norse world. Before a battle, before a major decision, before a journey of uncertain outcome, the lots were cast: marked pieces of wood or bone, drawn or thrown to reveal what could not otherwise be known. Perthro governs the moment of that drawing — the instant between intention and outcome, the hinge point where the known meets the unknown and whatever is going to happen becomes what happened. It is the rune of chance in the deepest sense: not random chance, but the intersection of your choices and intentions with the forces that operate outside your awareness and control.

In a reading, Perthro marks the presence of something concealed — information not yet available, outcomes not yet determined, a situation whose full shape will only become clear with time. Its appearance is neither good news nor bad news; it is an honest acknowledgment that this is a moment of genuine uncertainty, and that the appropriate response is openness rather than the forcing of premature conclusions. The rune invites a quality of alert receptivity: the readiness to receive what comes without having already decided what it will mean.

Perthro also governs the intuitive dimension of divination itself. When you draw runes, you are working in Perthro's territory — reaching into the unknown with a question, accepting what comes, reading the pattern that appears. The rune's presence in a spread sometimes points to the divination practice itself, suggesting that deeper or more patient work with the runes is called for before any decision is made.

Reversed, Perthro indicates a closing rather than an opening — secrets being withheld rather than revealed, the timing wrong for this particular inquiry, a need to step back from divination work and allow something to settle before looking again. It can occasionally signal an uncomfortable disclosure on its way: something hidden that is about to surface, whether or not you are ready for it.

Working with Perthro means cultivating comfort with not knowing — which is, for most people, a practice requiring considerable effort.

Algiz (*al-geez*)

The fifteenth rune looks like a hand raised in protection. Algiz — its name likely connected to the Proto-Germanic word for elk or for the concept of sacred protection — takes a form that reaches upward and outward in three directions: a vertical staff with two diagonal branches angling up toward the sky, suggesting both the antlers of a stag and the gesture of a figure calling on higher powers for aid. It is the rune of the guardian, the shield, the boundary that holds.

Algiz governs the interface between the human world and the wider field of forces that surround it. In Norse cosmology, the boundary between Midgard and the other worlds was porous and required active maintenance — not paranoia, but vigilance, the kind that comes from knowing where you stand and what you stand for. Algiz embodies this vigilance: not the fearful watchfulness of someone expecting attack, but the grounded alertness of someone whose protective awareness comes from a strong sense of their own position in the world. The rune is associated with the Valkyries — the choosers of the slain, figures who stand at the boundary between life and death, between the human and the divine, exercising discernment about who passes from one realm to the other.

In a reading, Algiz is often a welcome presence: it marks a period of protection, or indicates that the protective resources available to you — your own instincts, the support of people around you, the alignment of circumstances in your favor — are stronger than you may currently be aware of. It can also appear as a direct call to pay attention to your intuition about a situation, to trust the instinctive read that something is or is not safe before the rational analysis has caught up.

Reversed, Algiz points to vulnerability — defenses lowered at the wrong moment, a boundary that has been allowed to erode, the danger that comes from excessive trust in a situation or person that has not yet earned it. The reversal can also indicate that the defenses themselves have become the problem: excessive guard-edness that isolates rather than protects, the armoring that keeps out harm and keeps out nourishment with equal efficiency. Algiz reversed asks whether the protection strategy currently deployed is serving you or merely reinforcing a sense of threat that may be exaggerated.

The practice that Algiz supports most directly is the development of discernment — the capacity to distinguish what is genuinely threatening from what is merely unfamiliar, and to respond to each with appropriate rather than automatic behavior.

Sowilo (so-wee-lo)

The sixteenth rune is the sun. In its earliest forms, Sowilo appears as a simple zigzag or S-shape — the visual rendering of a lightning bolt or a ray of light, the path of energy moving through the world in the fastest and most direct way available to it. The sun in Norse cosmology was a goddess, Sol, who drove her chariot across the sky each day pursued by the great wolf Sköll, who would catch her only at Ragnarök. The daily crossing was not a given; it was a race, and the sun won it every day until the last day. Sowilo carries this quality: the victory that must be run for, the light that prevails not because darkness is weak but because the sun is strong.

Sowilo governs will, directed purpose, and the particular quality of clarity that comes when consciousness is fully aligned with what it is doing. Not the scattered brightness of diffuse energy, but the focused beam — the solar energy that, concentrated correctly, can ignite. When Sowilo appears in a reading, it marks a period of clarity and momentum, a time when effort and intention are working to-gether effectively, when the direction is right and the force behind it is real. It is a rune of success, but earned success: the victory that comes from the sustained application of genuine will.

The rune's association with honor is worth dwelling on. Sowilo in Norse tradition carried an ethical dimension alongside its energetic one. The sun reveals; it does not allow concealment. To be aligned with Sowilo is to be operating transparently, with integrity — to have the inner and outer aspects of your situation coherent with each other. When that coherence is present, the rune's energy moves freely. When it is absent — when there is a gap between how things appear and what is actually happening — Sowilo's quality of illumination tends to close down.

Sowilo carries no reversed meaning, which aligns it with Jera and Hagalaz as runes that represent cosmic forces too fundamental to invert. The sun does not have a shadow position. What changes is only your orientation to it. In readings, Sowilo's placement in a spread tells you where the clarity and momentum are currently available in the situation being examined.

As the last rune of Heimdall's Aett, Sowilo closes the cycle of disruption and transformation with an affirmation of earned light. The eight runes of this group have moved through destruction and necessity, stillness and harvest, the deep threshold of Eihwaz, the mystery of Perthro, the protection of Algiz — and they arrive here, at the rune of the sun after the long passage through difficulty. The light is real. You ran for it through a difficult stretch of ground. Sowilo confirms that the running was worth it.

The Third Aett: Tyr's Aett

Tyr is the god who gave his hand so that the world could be held together. When the gods needed to bind the wolf Fenrir — whose power was growing toward the magnitude that would, at Ragnarök, consume Odin himself — only the magical fetter Gleipnir could hold him. But Fenrir would not submit to binding unless one of the gods placed a hand in his mouth as a pledge of good faith. Every god understood what this meant: the wolf would be bound, and in the moment he realized it, the hand would be gone. Tyr stepped forward. He placed his right hand between Fenrir's jaws. The fetter held. Fenrir bit.

The story is one of the most compressed and resonant in Norse mythology. Tyr was the god of law and justice, of the ordered principles that make collective life possible. His sacrifice was not impulsive heroism — it was the deliberate acceptance of a personal cost for the sake of a larger necessity. The hand lost was the hand of a warrior, the hand that held the weapon. He gave up his capacity for certain kinds of individual power in order to preserve the structure that made all power meaningful.

The eight runes of Tyr's Aett carry this quality. They are the runes of integration — of the individual finding their place within larger structures of meaning, legacy, and relationship. Where Freyr's Aett built the foundations of a life and Heimdall's Aett broke them open through disruption and transformation, Tyr's Aett asks what you will do with what you have become. They are runes of maturity, not in the sense of age, but in the sense of depth — the depth that comes from having moved through difficulty and arrived at something you did not have before.

Tiwaz (*tee-wahz*)

The seventeenth rune is shaped like an arrow pointing straight up — a clean vertical line with two diagonal strokes angling downward from the tip, forming a spear or a direction marker. It is one of the most immediately legible forms in the Elder Futhark: something that points, that aims, that holds its direction regardless of what surrounds it. Tiwaz takes its name from the Proto-Germanic word for Tyr, and its shape was understood as the god's own symbol — the upward-pointing arm of a figure whose other arm was gone.

Tiwaz governs directed will, moral courage, and the kind of integrity that holds its shape under pressure. It is not the reckless courage of someone who has not considered the cost, but the deliberate courage of someone who has weighed what will be lost and chosen to proceed anyway, because the cause is worth it. The rune's association with the North Star — Polaris, the fixed point around which the other stars appear to rotate, the sailor's guide in the open ocean — gives it a quality of reliable orientation. Tiwaz is the thing you return to when the other landmarks are obscured: the inner north star, the value or principle that does not shift with circumstance.

In a reading, Tiwaz marks a moment requiring this kind of commitment. A decision that cannot be made from the middle ground, a situation in which the principled choice comes at a cost, a moment when personal sacrifice is the condition of genuine integrity. The rune does not sentimentalize what it asks. It simply points up-ward, indicating the direction, and leaves the moving to you. When Tiwaz appears in a spread alongside questions about jus-tice — legal matters, conflicts of principle, situations where something unfair has been done and must be addressed — it consistently favors the direct and honest approach over the strategic one.

Reversed, Tiwaz points to a failure of this directed will: cowardice masquerading as pragmatism, the abandonment of a principle because maintaining it became expensive, an ego overriding a deeper sense of what is right. The reversal can also indicate the exhaustion that comes from having held a position for too long without adequate support — the particular diminishment of someone who has been Tyr's stand-in for a situation that should have been shared. Tiwaz reversed asks whether you are genuine-ly committed to the direction you are pointing, or whether the arrow has been aimed by someone else's hand.

Working with Tiwaz means identifying, with some precision, what you actually stand for — not in the abstract, but in the specific conditions of the life you are currently living. The rune has no interest in beliefs that have never been tested.

Berkana (bear-kah-nah)

The eighteenth rune presents a shape found in nature and in the human body: two rounded lobes on a vertical staff, a form that suggests breasts, buds, or the twin halves of a seed beginning to open. Berkana's name comes from the Proto-Germanic word for birch, and the birch tree is exactly what the rune evokes — the first tree to send out green in spring, the pioneer species that colonizes cleared ground before the other trees arrive, the wood that was used across the Norse world for brooms, for cradles, and for the first writing surfaces of childhood.

Berkana governs beginnings, gestation, and the particular quality of care that allows new life to develop protected from forces that would overwhelm it before it is ready. It is the rune of the womb — not only in the literal sense but in every context where something vulnerable and unformed needs to be held safely while it becomes what it will be. A new project in its early stages, a relationship still finding its shape, an idea not yet ready for external judgment, a grief that needs to be tended quietly before it can be expressed. Berkana is the rune that asks: what do you need to protect here, and what conditions does it need to grow?

The birch tree's quality of concealment is part of Berkana's meaning. The birch does not announce itself; it arrives where it is needed and does its work quietly, stabilizing the soil, creating shade, enabling the seedlings of the larger trees to take root in its protection. Berkana's secrecy is not deception — it is the discretion of the midwife, who knows that certain processes require privacy to complete themselves, that premature exposure to scrutiny or judgment can damage what is being born.

In a reading, Berkana often marks the beginning of something — a new phase, a new relationship, a new creative endeavor — or signals that an existing situation needs more of this quality of nurturing attention than it is currently receiving. The rune is strongly associated with women and with the feminine principle in its generative dimension, but its applicability is not gendered: anyone in any situation can find themselves in a Berkana moment, called upon to provide the kind of patient, protective care that allows growth to proceed at its own pace.

Reversed, Berkana points to a disruption of this process — anxiety interfering with gestation, care withheld or withdrawn at a critical moment, the premature exposure of something not yet ready, or the refusal to protect what needs protecting because the effort seems too costly. The reversed rune can also indicate a situation in which growth has been prevented for so long that new energy can no longer find a way in. In either case, the question the rune asks is: what has been refused the care it needed, and what would it take to provide that care now?

Ehwaz (ay-wahz)

The nineteenth rune means horse. The shape of Ehwaz — two vertical strokes connected in their middles by a horizontal bar, like a letter H — suggests the bond between two parallel things, held together at the center. This is precisely what the rune governs: the relationship between a rider and their horse, which in Norse culture was among the closest and most significant bonds a person could maintain. A horse was not merely transport; it was a partner in every undertaking that required travel, and travel in the Norse world was rarely trivial.

Ehwaz governs all partnerships characterized by mutual trust, co-ordinated movement, and the kind of working relationship where each party's capability is enhanced by the presence of the other. The rider directs; the horse carries. But in a good partnership, this is not a hierarchy of domination — it is a dialogue of attunement, each responsive to the other's subtle signals, the whole moving more fluidly and more powerfully than either could alone. Ehwaz asks about this quality in every relationship it touches: is there genuine coordination here, or is one party carrying while the other merely holds the reins?

In a reading, Ehwaz marks movement and positive progression, particularly when that movement involves working with rather than against the other forces in a situation. For questions about partnerships — professional, romantic, creative — the rune asks whether the coordination between the parties is genuine, whether trust has been built through action rather than assumed, whether the relationship's movement is shared. For questions about transitions or journeys, it signals that the conditions for successful movement are in place, provided the coordination is maintained.

The rune's concern with trust is not abstract. Trust in Ehwaz terms is something demonstrated in the consistent quality of small decisions, in the accumulated record of showing up reliably over time. The horse-and-rider bond is not established in a day; it is built through repeated experience of mutual responsiveness. Ehwaz points toward this kind of trust and asks you to assess honestly how much of it is actually present in the situation being examined.

Reversed, Ehwaz indicates disharmony in a partnership, or movement blocked by a failure of coordination — mistrust that has not been named, a relationship in which the power distribution has become coercive rather than cooperative, a journey attempted before the ground was properly prepared. The reversed rune can also appear when restlessness is masquerading as momentum: the sense of needing to move without the clarity about where to go that would make the movement productive.

Mannaz (*man-ahz*)

The twentieth rune contains within its shape the form of Ehwaz expanded and made self-reflexive: two parallel vertical lines connected by crossed diagonals in the center, a form that looks like two figures facing each other or a single figure mirrored. Mannaz means human being — not any specific individual, but the human as a category, the creature that is defined precisely by its relationships with others of its kind. The rune's name is cognate with the English word "man" in its older, gender-neutral sense: the being who stands upright, who thinks, who uses language, who belongs to a community.

Mannaz governs the full complexity of human social existence — not only the pleasant dimensions of connection and cooperation, but the full range of what it means to be a creature whose identity is formed through relationship. The sense of self that knows itself partly through how others reflect it back. The capacity for reason and for self-deception in roughly equal measure. The longing for belonging and the fear of being absorbed. The intelligence that is the most distinctly human characteristic, and the blindness that intelligence enables when it is turned toward the project of self-justification.

In a reading, Mannaz asks about the quality of your current relationship with your own humanity — which is to say, with your own limitations, your own membership in a species that is simultaneously extraordinary and deeply flawed. The rune often appears when the situation being examined requires a degree of self-examination that has been avoided: a moment to step back from the story you have been telling about a situation and ask whether that story is genuinely accurate, or whether it has been shaped by needs and defenses that are operating below the level of conscious awareness.

The rune's connection to Mímir's Well — the source of wisdom that Odin sacrificed his eye to access — places it in the territory of deep, costly knowledge. Mannaz is not the rune of comfortable self-knowledge. It is the rune of the kind of honest self-appraisal that requires setting aside the version of yourself you prefer to present, and looking at what is actually there.

Reversed, Mannaz points to the shadow dimensions of human social existence: manipulation, self-deception, the isolation that comes from having withdrawn from authentic connection, the arrogance that mistakes one perspective for universal truth. The reversed rune often marks a moment of significant self-delusion — a situation in which the internal narrative has become so shaped by defensive needs that it can no longer accurately reflect what is happening. The invitation is not self-punishment but a genuine willingness to see more clearly.

Laguz (*lah-gooz*)

The twenty-first rune is water. Laguz — its name from the Proto-Germanic word for lake or sea — presents a shape that flows: a vertical line with a diagonal stroke angling down to the right, suggesting something moving, something that follows the path available to it rather than the path it might prefer. Water in Norse cosmology was both the element of life and the element of the unknown. The sea was the route to everywhere and the source of the storms that made everywhere dangerous. The rivers were the roads that connected inland communities to the wider world and, in the deep places, held things that could not be clearly seen.

Laguz governs the unconscious — not in the clinical sense, but in the experiential sense: the part of your inner life that is not directly available to deliberate thought, that communicates in feelings and images and intuitions rather than in the language of argument. The rune governs dreams, the psychic dimension, the capacity to sense what is present in a situation before the rational mind has assembled the evidence. It is associated with the feminine principle in its deepest, most fluid form: not the structured, generative feminine of Berkana, but the formless, receptive, sometimes dangerous feminine of the deep water.

In a reading, Laguz calls attention to the felt dimension of the situation being examined. It asks what you sense, as distinct from what you think — what the body knows before the mind has processed it, what the quiet persistent feeling in the background is trying to tell you before it gets overridden by more socially acceptable conclusions. The rune is a consistent advocate for trusting your intuition, particularly in situations where the rational analysis is inconclusive or where your instinctive response is significantly at odds with what seems logical.

The rune also carries the quality of flow — the water's capacity to find its way around obstacles, to take the shape of whatever contains it while remaining essentially itself. Laguz in a reading sometimes asks not whether you can force a situation in a particular direction but whether you can release the grip of forced direction and allow the situation to move as it needs to. Going with the current rather than fighting it. Allowing what wants to dissolve to dissolve, and what wants to deepen to deepen.

Reversed, Laguz speaks to stagnation — water that has stopped flowing, intuition that has been suppressed or overridden until it has gone underground, the emotional backlog of feelings that have not been acknowledged and are now creating pressure from below. The reversed rune can also indicate a situation in which the pull of the unconscious is too strong — where the boundaries of the self are dissolving in ways that are not chosen but imposed, where what feels like receptivity is actually a dangerous kind of passivity.

Working with Laguz means developing a practice of attending to your inner life with something like the patient, non-judgmental attention of a naturalist observing water: noting what moves, what pools, what gets dammed, what finds its way through.

Ingwaz (*ing-wahz*)

The twenty-second rune is sometimes rendered as a diamond — four diagonal lines meeting at right angles to form a closed shape — and sometimes as a diamond stacked on a diamond, two joined lozenges. Either way, the form suggests something complete in itself, sealed, containing its energy rather than dispersing it. Ingwaz takes its name from Ing, an ancient Germanic deity of fertility and the land, a figure whose cultic worship predates the Viking Age and whose name survives embedded in place names and in the English suffix -*ing* that, as the original text notes with quiet accuracy, indicates ongoing action.

Ingwaz governs gestation of a particular kind: the gathering and containment of energy before its release. It is the seed in winter, holding within a hard outer shell everything required for the tree it will become, waiting for the conditions that will allow that potential to unfold. The rune is associated with a period of internal preparation — the work that happens before the work, the accumulation that makes the sudden breakthrough possible. In physics terms, Ingwaz is potential energy: stored, concentrated, not yet expressed.

The rune's connection to the cycle of sacrifice and regeneration gives it a quality that the seed metaphor also holds: something must end — must be given over, must in a real sense die — before what is stored within it can become something new. The old form is the vessel; the new form is what the vessel releases when it has completed its purpose. Ingwaz does not grieve the old form. It is wholly oriented toward what the transformation makes possible.

In a reading, Ingwaz marks a moment of internal completion — the sense that a phase of preparation or gestation is nearing its end, that the conditions for release are approaching. It can appear when a long effort is finally about to yield its results, when an internal shift that has been developing below the level of conscious awareness is about to become visible, when something that has been held in readiness is finally ready to move. The rune carries no reversed position: the seed does not reverse. The potential it contains either meets the conditions for its release or it waits.

Working with Ingwaz calls for patience with the invisible. The rune asks you to trust that the work you cannot see being done is nonetheless being done — that gestation is real even when it produces no external evidence, that the quiet periods in a life or a project are not empty but full in a way that does not yet show.

Dagaz (*dah-gahz*)

The twenty-third rune is dawn — specifically, the threshold between night and day, the precise moment of transformation when darkness becomes light. Dagaz presents a shape that enacts its meaning: two triangles meeting at their points in the center, each one opening in the opposite direction, neither one dominant, the balance between them the whole point. It is the rune of the moment that contains both what is ending and what is beginning, neither yet the past nor the future, but the infinitely thin present where they exchange.

Dagaz governs breakthrough and awakening — the quality of transformation that is sudden rather than gradual, the insight that arrives complete rather than building incrementally, the moment of clarity after a long period of confusion when everything that was obscure resolves into a new and comprehensive understanding. Where Jera governs the harvest earned by patient seasonal labor, Dagaz governs the dawn that simply arrives — irreversible, transforming, equally unearned and undeniable. You do not cultivate a dawn. You are present for it, or you miss it.

The rune's quality of non-duality is among its most significant attributes. At the precise moment of dawn, it is neither night nor day — it is the threshold where both coexist and neither is complete. Dagaz holds this paradoxical space as a permanent condition rather than a passing anomaly. The rune suggests that the highest clarity is available not when one side defeats the other, but when both are held simultaneously, when the apparent opposition between them resolves into a larger understanding that contains them both.

In a reading, Dagaz marks a significant turning point — a moment when a new level of clarity or consciousness is becoming available, when something that has long been obscure is about to become visible, when a transformation that has been building reaches the point of its completion. The rune has no reversed position, like the dawn itself: the transition it marks always moves in the same direction. What changes is only whether you are facing it or turned away.

Dagaz is the rune of the mystic moment, the sudden apprehension of connection and meaning that the Norse understood as Odin's gift: the capacity for the human mind to touch, however briefly, a level of awareness that transcends its ordinary operating conditions. The rune does not promise this experience will last. It confirms that it is available, and that your presence for it — the quality of attention you bring to the threshold — is what makes the difference.

Othala (oh-thah-lah)

The twenty-fourth and final rune closes the cycle by returning to where it began, but changed. Othala — its name from the Proto-Germanic word for ancestral estate, inherited property, the home that belongs to a family across generations — presents a shape that combines the upward-pointing form of Tiwaz with a horizontal base: an arrow grounded, a direction that is also a foundation. The rune governs inheritance in the fullest sense: not only property and land, but the accumulated wisdom, character, and consequence of all the generations that preceded you.

Fehu, the first rune, governed the wealth acquired in a single lifetime — mobile, current, circulating. Othala governs the wealth that cannot be spent and cannot be earned in one generation: the qualities passed down through blood and culture and story, the patterns that express themselves in a family line whether or not the people carrying them are aware of them. This inheritance works in both directions. The gifts of your ancestors come with you into every situation you encounter. So do the unresolved patterns, the wounds that were never healed, the choices that were made and never examined. Othala asks you to attend to both with equal honesty.

In a reading, Othala asks about the relationship between where you come from and where you are going — about which aspects of your inheritance are genuinely yours to carry forward and which are patterns that belong to an earlier time and no longer serve the life you are trying to build. The rune does not romanticize ancestry; it takes it seriously, which is different. To be a good ancestor to those who come after you, it is necessary to understand what you received from those who came before, to integrate what is valuable and consciously release what is not.

The rune's connection to homeland and community extends beyond family in the narrow sense. Othala governs every form of belonging that is both given and earned: the culture that formed you, the community you are part of, the landscape that has shaped your sense of what the world is. These are inheritances too, and the rune asks the same questions of them: what do you carry from them that is genuinely yours, and what have you taken on by default that deserves examination?

Reversed, Othala speaks to the shadow of inherited patterns — prejudice, dysfunction, the transmission of unexamined wounds from one generation to the next, the clinging to forms of belonging that have become exclusive or harmful. The reversed rune often marks a moment when the inherited pattern has become a limitation rather than a resource, when the house that should be a home has become a prison. The invitation is not to reject the inheritance but to examine it: to distinguish what is living in it from what has died, and to carry forward only what genuinely nourishes the life ahead.

Othala closing the Elder Futhark and Fehu opening it is one of the sequence's most deliberate gestures. The wealth you earn in this life becomes the inheritance you leave behind. The inheritance you received shaped the conditions in which you earn. The cycle is not a repetition — each turn of it adds to what is being passed forward. This is the final teaching of the twenty-four runes, delivered quietly, in the shape of a grounded arrow pointing home.

The Magic of Runes: Galdr, Seidr, and the Völva

T he word the Norse used most broadly for magic was *fjölkyngi* — great knowledge. The term is built from the verb *kunna*, which meant to know, to understand, to hold something in memory by heart, to be intimately familiar with the old traditions. Magic, in this framework, was not a supernatural power set apart from the world of knowledge and craft. It was knowledge of a particular depth and kind — knowledge of the forces operating in and through things, knowledge of how those forces could be reached and worked with. A magician was, above all, someone who knew more than ordinary people knew, and who had paid the cost that such knowing required.

This understanding is worth holding onto as we move from the symbolic meanings of the runes into the question of how they were actually used. The Norse did not draw a clean line between divination, magic, and spiritual practice. These were aspects of a single field of activity, differentiated by technique and context rather than by category. What follows is an account of the three primary traditions within which runic practice was embedded — *galdr*, the specifically runic magic of sound and inscription; *seidr*, the broader shamanic tradition associated most closely with Freyja; and the *völva*, the wise woman whose role encompassed both and whose practice represented the most formalized expression of Norse magical knowledge.

Galdr: The Magic of the Chanted Rune

The word *galdr* derives from the Old Norse verb *gala*, meaning to crow or to sing in a high, piercing voice — the cry of a bird, or the particular quality of sound produced when a runic name is not merely spoken but intoned with full intention. Galdr was the practice of working with runes through voice: chanting the names of individual runes, combining them into sequences, singing them over objects, over wounds, over the bodies of the sick, over weapons before battle. The sound was not incidental to the magic. The sound was the magic, or a large part of it — the vocal activation of the force that the rune represented, the sending of that force into the world through the medium of the human voice.

The *Hávamál* describes eighteen magical chants that Odin commands after winning the runes, each one capable of producing a specific effect: reversing a curse, calming a storm at sea, extinguishing fire, restoring the slain to life, binding enemies, winning the love of a woman, shielding a friend in battle. The list is less a recipe collection than a demonstration of scope — an indication that galdr, when fully mastered, provided access to the full range of forces operating in the world. In practice, most galdr work was more modest and more focused: a single rune chanted with concentration over a specific object or situation, directing the rune's energy toward a clear purpose.

The physical dimension of galdr was inscription. To chant a rune's name while carving or painting its form was to work on two channels simultaneously — the sonic and the visual, the voice and the hand — and the combination was understood to be significantly more powerful than either alone. Runic amulets found at archaeological sites across Scandinavia and the Germanic world often bear evidence of both: the carved form and, inferred from context, the chanting that would have accompanied the carving. Objects intended for healing or protection were not simply marked; they were activated through a process of focused making, in which the craftsperson's voice and intention were embedded in the object alongside the physical inscription.

The runes of the *Hávamál*'s eighteen chants are not named explicitly in the poem — Odin speaks of what the chants can accomplish without specifying which runes carry which power. This is consistent with how galdr knowledge appears to have been transmitted: not as a fixed code to be memorized, but as a practice built from long familiarity with the runes' individual energies and how they could be combined. The practitioner who knew that Algiz governed protection, that Tiwaz governed directed will, and that Sowilo governed the force of solar clarity could combine them in a chant for a warrior going into battle in ways that no written manual could fully specify in advance. The knowledge was held in the body as much as in the mind, accumulated through years of working with individual runes in individual situations until the combinations became as natural as spoken grammar.

This principle extends to the bindrune — a composite form in which two or more runic shapes are merged into a single symbol, their forces combined into a focused unit. A bindrune for a specific purpose does not simply add its component runes together; it creates something new from their interaction, a symbol whose meaning emerges from the relationship between the forces it holds rather than from their sum. Making a bindrune requires knowing not only what individual runes mean but how they speak to each other — a knowledge that comes from sustained practice and a quality of attention that goes well beyond learning definitions. The best bindrunes are not designed intellectually but arrived at through a process of holding the desired outcome alongside the runes that address it, waiting for the forms to show how they want to sit together.

The Egil Story

Egil's Saga, one of the great Icelandic family sagas, contains a passage that remains one of the most vivid illustrations of runic magic in the literary record. Egil Skallagrímsson — farmer, warrior, and skald, a man whose relationship with the runes was bound up with his poetic gift as well as his practical intelligence — stops at a farmhouse while traveling. The farmer's daughter lies gravely ill, wasting in a way that no ordinary remedy has been able to address.

Egil examines the girl's bed and finds, concealed beneath the mattress, a piece of whalebone covered in runic carvings. He identifies the carvings immediately as the source of the girl's condition — not because runic inscription is inherently harmful, but because these particular runes are wrong. The carver was a young man from a neighboring farm who had attempted to craft a love charm for the girl, working from partial knowledge. The runes he cut were not merely impotent; they were, in Egil's assessment, dangerous in the specific way that a misdirected force is dangerous: not evil in intent, but catastrophic in effect because the practitioner did not know what he was doing.

Egil scrapes off the inscription, burns the whalebone, and then carves a new set of runes — correct ones, oriented toward healing rather than toward the confused desire of the young man's original attempt. He places the new inscription near the girl. She recovers.

The story encodes several things at once. It confirms that runic knowledge was understood to be genuinely powerful — powerful enough to cause serious harm when misapplied. It establishes the distinction between the rune-user who knows what they are doing and the one who merely knows the shapes of the letters. And it places runic competence in the same category as any skilled craft:

not a mysterious privilege dispensed from above, but a discipline with real stakes and real consequences for sloppy workmanship. Egil does not perform a counter-curse. He corrects bad work with good work, the way a skilled carpenter might correct a faulty joint. The runes themselves are not evil. The error is human.

The saga also contains an earlier runic episode that receives less attention but is equally instructive. At a feast where Egil suspects the drinking horn has been poisoned, he scratches runes onto the horn and smears them with his blood, after which the horn shatters. The episode assumes that Egil's runic knowledge was sufficiently advanced that this response — a kind of runic testing or breaking of the vessel — was the natural first move for a man of his competence when he suspected magical interference with food or drink. Runic practice, in Egil's world, was not reserved for solemn occasions. It was a skill available in ordinary situations, ready to be deployed the way a craftsperson deploys their tools, with economy and without ceremony.

Seidr: The Shamanic Tradition

Alongside galdr — and sometimes overlapping with it, sometimes operating in entirely different registers — was *seidr*, the practice most closely associated with Freyja and with the broader shamanic traditions of the Norse world. The word's etymology points toward binding or entwining: seidr was understood as a form of engagement with the threads of fate, the capacity to perceive them, to move along them, to influence how they ran. Where galdr worked primarily through voice and inscription, seidr worked through trance — a deliberate alteration of consciousness that allowed the practitioner to move between the ordinary world and the deeper layers of reality underlying it.

Freyja was the foremost seidr practitioner among the gods, and it was from her that Odin learned the art — a transmission that the sources treat as significant, even slightly scandalous, since seidr was associated with female practice and with a kind of self-dissolution that the warrior ethic found uncomfortable. Odin's willingness to learn it anyway is consistent with his defining characteristic: the absolute refusal to leave any significant domain of knowledge unvisited, regardless of what it cost him in dignity or social positioning.

The practice of seidr as described in the sagas involved the practitioner — typically a völva, a staff-bearing wise woman — entering a trance state, often with the aid of a specific seat, particular garments, and the singing of *varðlokur*, calling songs performed by assistants to draw the spirits necessary for the working. In this trance state, the völva could perceive fate, answer questions about the future, locate missing persons or animals, identify the causes of illness, and interact with the non-human intelligences that populated the Norse cosmological landscape. The working was communal: the völva was the center of a ritual that required the participation and the vocal support of the community she served.

The *Eiríks saga rauða* — Erik the Red's Saga — contains one of the most detailed accounts of a seidr working in the saga literature. A völva named Þorbjörg arrives at a Greenland farm during a famine and hard winter. She is received with formal ceremony: a special high seat prepared for her, particular foods prepared according to tradition, and the community assembled to provide the singing she requires. The following morning she delivers her prophecy, addressing each person's questions in turn. The account reads less like a supernatural performance and more like a professional consultation: the völva's knowledge and the community's ritual support together create the conditions in which the deeper perception becomes available.

Seidr's relationship to the runes was not always direct, but the underlying logic was continuous with galdr: the practitioner was working with the forces that the runes mapped, attempting to reach and influence the deeper patterns of which human events were the surface expression. A völva reading fate was engaged with the same field that the Norns operated in when they carved their determinations into Yggdrasil's bark. The runes were one language for this field; seidr was another way of entering it.

The Völva: Keeper of the Old Knowledge

Of all the figures in the Norse magical tradition, the völva — whose name means staff-carrier — is the one whose role most fully encompasses what magic meant in that world. She was not a specialist in one technique; she was a practitioner of the full range of indigenous wisdom, holding in a single person the knowledge of plants and healing, the ability to enter trance and read fate, the authority to advise on matters of community welfare, and the specialized skills of runic inscription and magical working. She moved between settlements as a valued visitor, her arrival an occasion for formal ceremony, her readings sought by farmers, chieftains, and kings.

The sagas treat the völva with a particular mixture of reverence and unease that is itself revealing. She held a kind of power that did not fit neatly into the categories that Norse society otherwise used to organize authority — she was not a warrior, not a political leader, not a priest in any formal sense. Her power came from knowledge, from the specific quality of attention she had developed, from the relationships she maintained with forces that ordinary people could not access. This made her indispensable and, at the same time, slightly outside the structures through which other forms of authority were legitimized.

Archaeological evidence has begun to fill in what the sagas describe. Several graves identified as belonging to völvas have been excavated across Scandinavia and beyond, recognizable by a characteristic assemblage of objects: a iron staff, typically about a meter long and sometimes decorated; unusual collections of animal bones and seeds; objects from distant places suggesting extensive travel; in some cases, cannabis seeds thought to have been used to induce altered states. The graves are remarkable for their richness and for the effort clearly expended on them, confirming the sagas' account of the völva as a figure of considerable status. One particularly striking example, found at Fyrkat in Denmark and dating to the late tenth century, was buried with what appears to be a complete ritual kit — the evidence of an entire professional practice interred with its practitioner.

When Christianity arrived in Scandinavia, the völva's position became precarious in a new way. The traditions she embodied — the trance practices, the communication with non-human intelligences, the reading of fate — were precisely what the new religion condemned most forcefully. Some scholars argue that the European figure of the witch is, in significant part, the völva surviving under a different name and a different valuation: the same knowledge, the same practices, the same capacity for movement between the worlds, now reframed as diabolical rather than sacred. The continuity is imperfect and contested, but the structural resemblance is difficult to dismiss.

Runic Magic in a Modern Context

The question of how to work with runic magic today does not have a single answer, and anyone who offers one with too much confidence is probably selling something. What the tradition provides is a set of principles, a vocabulary of forces, and a collection of techniques that can be approached with varying degrees of formality depending on your temperament and your practice.

At the most accessible end, galdr requires nothing more than a rune, your voice, and your attention. Sitting quietly with a specific rune, sounding its name aloud slowly and repeatedly, attending to what arises in the body and in the mind as the sound moves through you — this is a genuine practice, connected to the tradition's oldest layer, requiring no special equipment and no prior initiation. The rune's name is the rune's energy rendered in sound. Giving it your voice is a form of invitation.

Inscription — carving, painting, drawing — extends the practice into the physical world. An amulet made with clear intention, its rune carved while its name is sounded, its purpose held in mind throughout the making, is an object in which the galdr principle is embedded. The tradition held that the material mattered: certain woods, certain metals, certain stones were understood to carry energies that would support or amplify particular runic forces. Working with these correspondences is not required, but attending to them tends to deepen the practice.

The deeper practices — bindrune work, extended galdr sequences, anything that approaches the seidr tradition of trance and journey — benefit from a foundation in the simpler work. The rune diary recommended in the introduction is not a beginner's exercise to be discarded once you feel you know the runes. It is the foundation on which every more advanced practice stands. The völva's authority came from years of accumulated attention, from the relationship she had built with the forces she worked with over a long practice. The same principle applies now, on whatever scale you are working.

What connects the ancient tradition to whatever practice you develop today is the underlying conviction that the runes are not inert symbols. They are condensed relationships between the human mind and the forces that structure existence. Working with them — in any form, with any degree of formality — is an engagement with something real. That engagement is what the tradition has always been, from the Norns carving fate into the World Tree to the person who draws a rune from a bag on an ordinary Tuesday morning and sits with what it says.

The Art of Runic Divination

D ivination is an old word with a simple root: *divinare*, to be inspired by a god, to foresee. At its center is the idea that there are forms of knowledge not available through ordinary observation and reasoning, and that certain practices can create the conditions in which that knowledge becomes accessible. The runes are one of the oldest known instruments for this kind of practice in the Northern European tradition, and their use in divination is inseparable from the understanding of what runes are: not arbitrary symbols, but condensed relationships between human consciousness and the forces that structure experience.

This is worth distinguishing from fortune-telling, because the two are genuinely different things. Fortune-telling offers information about what will happen. Divination, in the deeper sense, offers a quality of perception about what is — what is present in a situation, what forces are active, what patterns are at work beneath the surface of events. The rune drawn in the morning does not tell you what will happen today. It offers a lens through which to see today more clearly, a focal point for the quality of attention you bring to what unfolds. The difference matters practically: it shifts the relationship with the runes from one of passive reception to one of active engagement.

What You Are Working With

When you cast runes, you are working with a system that has three distinct layers. The first is the symbolic layer: the meanings associated with each of the twenty-four runes, their associations, their names, their connections to Norse myth and cosmology. This is the layer that can be learned from a book, and learning it is necessary. But it is not sufficient.

The second layer is the intuitive layer: your own developing capacity to sense what a particular rune means in a particular context, for a particular question, on a particular day. The same rune drawn in response to two different questions means different things. The meanings described in Part Three of this book are starting points, not fixed definitions. Over time, as you work with the runes consistently, you will find that certain runes speak to you in ways that go beyond the recorded meanings — that they develop a kind of personal resonance, a vocabulary specific to your life and your patterns of attention. This is not deviation from the tradition. It is what the tradition is for.

The third layer is the relational layer: what happens in the encounter between your question and the rune that appears. The Norse understanding of divination was not that a rune chosen at random had a fixed message to deliver. It was that the rune that came forward in response to a genuine question had been, in some sense, called — that the relationship between your inner state, the energy of the question, and the forces the rune represents creates a specific meaning that belongs to that moment and cannot be fully replicated in another. This is why rune readings for the same question on different days can yield genuinely different results. The situation has changed, even if its surface appearance has not.

Preparing for a Reading

The quality of a rune reading is significantly shaped by the quality of attention brought to it. This does not require elaborate ritual — it requires honesty and stillness, which are sometimes harder to achieve than elaborate ritual.

Before drawing runes, it helps to spend a few minutes becoming genuinely quiet. This means setting aside the running commentary of whatever occupied your mind immediately before — the errands, the unresolved conversations, the plans being made. The runes respond to what is actually present in you, not to what you think you should be concerned with, and the gap between these two things can be significant. A few slow, deliberate breaths are usually enough to create some distance between the surface noise and whatever lies underneath it.

The question you bring to a reading deserves equal care. Vague questions tend to produce vague readings — not because the runes are incapable of precision, but because an unclear question reflects an unclear relationship with the situation being examined. "What should I do about my job?" is less useful than "What is the most important thing I am not seeing clearly about my current work situation?" The more precisely you can identify what you are actually asking, the more specifically the runes can respond.

It is also worth noting that certain questions are not well suited to rune divination. Questions that seek a simple yes or no answer — "Will this relationship work out?" — tend to miss the point of what runes offer. Questions that place the agency entirely outside yourself — "What will happen?" rather than "What do I need to understand?" — similarly misuse the instrument. The runes are most useful when the question is genuinely open, when you are asking not to have your preferred outcome confirmed but to perceive something you have not yet perceived.

The Merkstave

Before describing the specific methods of reading, the question of the reversed rune — the *merkstave* — deserves its own attention, because it is one of the more misunderstood aspects of runic divination.

Merkstave means, roughly, "dark stake" in Old Norse — a sign pointing toward shadow. When a rune appears upside down or reversed in a reading, its energy is understood to be present but distorted, blocked, or expressing itself through its shadow dimension rather than its primary quality. This does not mean the reversed rune is simply "bad news." It means the force the rune represents is at work in a way that is constrained, misdirected, or asking for conscious attention before it can move freely.

Fehu reversed does not mean "you will lose money." It means the energy of circulation and abundance has stalled somewhere, and understanding where it has stalled is the useful information. Tiwaz reversed does not mean "you will fail." It means the directed will and integrity that Tiwaz represents is not currently operating cleanly — perhaps because of competing pressures, perhaps because of a compromise that has been made without full acknowledgment, perhaps because the direction being pursued is not genuinely yours.

Reading the merkstave well requires the same quality of attention as reading the upright rune — perhaps more, because the shadow dimension is by definition less visible and more uncomfortable to look at directly. Some practitioners choose not to work with reversed runes at all, reading all runes in their upright position. This is a legitimate choice, particularly early in a practice, and it does not prevent good readings. But the reversed position, worked with honestly, tends to produce some of the most instructive results a reading can offer.

Methods of Reading

The single rune. The most fundamental practice: one rune drawn from the bag, held in the hand, attended to. For a daily practice, this is the foundation. It is also underestimated. A single rune, drawn with a clear question and sat with patiently for several minutes — noticing what arises in the body, what images come, what the rune's name sounds like when you say it aloud, what connections suggest themselves — produces more useful information than many more elaborate readings conducted without real attention. The daily rune practice described in the introduction is this: one rune, every morning, followed by a day of noticing where its energy appears, followed by a few minutes of writing in the evening about what you observed.

The three-rune spread. Three runes drawn and placed in sequence — most commonly representing past, present, and future; or situation, action, outcome; or what was, what is, what is becoming. The three-rune spread is the workhorse of runic divination, versatile enough to address almost any question and simple enough to be read clearly without extensive experience. The relationships between the three runes matter as much as the individual meanings: a rune of disruption in the past position and a rune of harvest in the future position tells a coherent story. A rune of stillness in the present flanked by runes of movement in past and future tells a different one.

The five-rune spread. An expansion of the three-rune structure, typically adding two runes: one representing hidden factors or unconscious influences, and one representing the best possible outcome if current energies are fully engaged. The five-rune spread is particularly useful when a situation feels more complex than three positions can hold, or when there is a strong sense that something relevant is operating below the surface of the question.

The nine-rune cast. Nine runes drawn from the bag and scattered onto a casting cloth or flat surface. Only the runes that fall face up are read; those face down are set aside. The runes are interpreted not only individually but in terms of their positions — which are closest to the center of the cloth, which near the edges, which are grouped together, which are isolated. This is the most fluid and most demanding of the common reading methods, requiring the practitioner to synthesize multiple data points without the scaffolding of predetermined positions. It produces readings of considerable depth and complexity when done well, and confusing noise when done carelessly. It is not the place to start, but it becomes available naturally as your relationship with the runes develops.

The runic cross. Six runes in a cross pattern, modeled loosely on the Celtic cross spread used in tarot: the central rune representing the core of the situation, a rune crossing it representing the primary challenge or complicating force, and four surrounding runes representing the past, the future, the querent's current stance, and the likely outcome. This spread works well for questions involving relationships or decisions where multiple perspectives need to be held simultaneously.

Reading the Spread

Once runes are drawn and placed, the reading begins — and this is where the second and third layers described at the start of this chapter become essential. The individual meanings of each rune are your starting point. The relationships between them are where the real reading happens.

Look at the spread as a whole before analyzing individual positions. What is the overall quality of the runes present? Are they predominantly runes associated with disruption and challenge, or runes associated with movement and clarity? Is there a rune that stands out immediately — one whose presence surprises you, or one that produces a strong physical response? Start there. The rune that draws your attention first is usually doing so for a reason.

Then attend to relationships. When Hagalaz appears alongside Sowilo, the combination speaks of disruption giving way to clarity — the storm that precedes a clearer sky. When Isa appears alongside Jera, it speaks of stillness before harvest — the period of waiting that the cycle requires before the results of previous effort can be gathered. These are not fixed rules; they are starting points for the kind of intuitive synthesis that develops with practice.

Pay attention to your physical responses throughout the reading. A sense of recognition when a particular rune appears — a felt sense of "yes, that's exactly it" — is information. So is resistance: the rune whose meaning you find yourself wanting to argue with or reframe is often the one carrying the message you most need. The runes say what they say regardless of whether it is convenient.

On Accuracy and Interpretation

Runic divination is not infallible, and claiming otherwise would be a disservice. The runes reflect what is present — the energies active in a situation, the patterns operating in a life — but the interpretation of what is present is a human act, subject to human limitations. Wishful thinking distorts readings. Fear distorts readings. The desire to hear a particular thing distorts readings. This is why the honest preparation described earlier matters: not because it makes you psychic, but because it reduces the noise that makes the signal harder to hear.

The runes also work on a timeframe that is not always the one you bring to them. A reading about a situation that resolves itself over months may look confusing if you expect resolution by next week. One of the most useful practices a rune reader can develop is keeping records — noting what was drawn in response to which questions, and returning to those notes at intervals to see what the runes were pointing toward that was not yet visible at the time of the reading. The accuracy of runic divination often becomes clear in retrospect, which is itself an instruction in the kind of patience the runes consistently ask for.

Finally: the runes are a tool for perception, not a replacement for judgment. Whatever a reading shows you, the decisions remain yours. The rune does not tell you what to do. It tells you what to see. What you do with what you see is entirely, irreversibly your own responsibility — and this, in the Norse understanding, was not a limitation of divination but its whole point.

Building Your Practice

There is a particular kind of book about spiritual practice that describes everything except how to actually do it. It covers history, philosophy, symbolism, and method in careful detail, and then ends — leaving the reader informed but unclear about what Tuesday morning looks like when they sit down with their rune bag and no one is watching. This chapter is an attempt to close that gap.

Everything in the preceding chapters has been preparation for this. The history gives the runes their context. The mythology gives them their depth. The detailed descriptions of all twenty-four symbols give you a vocabulary. The chapters on magic and divination give you a sense of what working with that vocabulary looks like. What remains is the question of how to weave these things into a practice that is genuinely yours — not a performance of runic expertise, not an imitation of what you think someone else's practice should look like, but a living engagement with the runes that develops over time and becomes, gradually, part of how you move through your life.

The Rune Set

Before anything else, you need runes you can work with physically. This sounds obvious, but the choice matters more than it might appear, because the object you use carries its own relationship with you over time.

You can buy a set. Rune sets made from wood, stone, ceramic, glass, or bone are widely available, and many of them are well-made objects that work well for the purpose. If you buy, choose something that feels right in your hand — that has a weight and texture you are comfortable holding, whose surface communicates the shape of each rune clearly when you feel it without looking. The tactile dimension of rune work is not incidental. The hand knows things.

You can also make a set, and there is a genuine tradition behind this choice. The Norse understanding of runic work was that the making was part of the activation — that the runes carved by your own hand in your own wood carried something that a purchased object could not. Making a set is time-consuming and requires some basic tools, but it does not require extraordinary skill. A set of twenty-four wooden discs, each one sanded smooth and inscribed with a burned or carved rune, made over a period of days with some attention to the process, is a more powerful working tool than most commercially produced alternatives, not because of any mystical property of hand-making, but because of what you learn in the making. By the time you have worked through all twenty-four runes with a carving tool, thinking about each one carefully enough to render it accurately, you know the alphabet in your hands as well as in your mind.

Whatever set you use, keep it in a bag or pouch — something that holds the runes together, that allows you to draw from them without looking. The bag creates a threshold: the runes inside it are, in a small and practical sense, in a different space from the ordinary objects around them. This distinction is useful.

The Rune Journal

The introduction to this book described my own early practice: one rune each morning, notes each evening, attention throughout the day to how the rune's energy appeared. I have recommended this approach throughout, and I want to be more specific here about what it actually involves, because "keep a journal" is advice that sounds simple and often fails in practice for entirely preventable reasons.

The journal does not need to be elaborate. A small notebook kept on the same surface as your rune bag — visible, accessible, not stored away somewhere — is ideal. The entry for each day needs only a few components: the date, the rune drawn, any immediate associations or responses you noticed when you drew it, and then, in the evening or whenever you return to it, a brief account of how the rune appeared during the day.

That last part is where the real learning happens, and it requires a particular quality of attention. When you draw Raidho in the morning and then notice, in the afternoon, that you are having a conversation about a decision that requires choosing a direction, the connection between the rune and the event is information. When you draw Isa and then find the day characterized by a frustrating inability to move forward on anything you try to accomplish, that is also information. When you draw Gebo and the day feels entirely disconnected from themes of exchange and gift — that is information too, and worth noting, because the rune you drew and the day you lived are not always obviously linked, and the discrepancy is often as instructive as the correspondence.

Over time, the journal becomes your personal runic reference — more specific and more useful than any published guide, because it records how these symbols speak to you, in the language of your particular life. You will notice patterns. Certain runes will appear repeatedly during periods with identifiable characteristics. Certain runes will consistently speak to you in ways that differ from the standard meanings, or that extend them in directions particular to your situation. This accumulated record is the foundation of any more advanced runic work you choose to undertake.

A few practical points. Do not draw the rune and then immediately read everything you can find about it before sitting with your own first response. The initial reaction — before the intellectual overlay, before you remember what the books say — is often the most accurate. Write it down first. Then, if you want to consult other sources, you can bring that material into dialogue with your own response rather than substituting it for one.

Keep the entries short enough that you actually write them. A practice that requires thirty minutes of writing per day will fail within a week for most people. A practice that requires five minutes will survive almost anything.

Working with a Single Rune

Alongside the daily rune journal, there is a different kind of work that goes deeper into individual symbols: the deliberate, extended meditation on a single rune over a period of days or weeks. This is how you build the kind of intimate knowledge of a rune that the journal practice introduces but cannot fully develop.

Choose one rune. Spend a week with it — not drawing it every day, but keeping it with you. Place it somewhere visible in your living or working space. Pick it up when you pass it. Hold it in your hand for a few minutes each day, attending to its form, its weight, its feel, sounding its name aloud slowly and noticing what the name produces in the body. Read what different sources say about it. Draw the rune's shape yourself, repeatedly, on paper, on the back of your hand, in the air. Notice when its energy appears in your daily experience, and when it notably does not appear.

This kind of extended engagement with a single rune is not a technique with a specific outcome. It is a relationship-building practice, and like all relationship-building, it works through accumulated time and attention rather than through any single dramatic encounter. After spending a week with Uruz in this way, you will know Uruz in a qualitatively different way than you did before — not because you learned more facts about it, but because you spent time in its company.

Reading for Yourself

There is a persistent idea in some divination traditions that you cannot read accurately for yourself — that the proximity of your own desires and fears to the question makes objective perception impossible. There is a version of this that is true: wishful thinking distorts readings, and readings about situations you are very strongly invested in require extra care. But the wholesale outsourcing of your own divination to others is a misunderstanding of what rune work is for. The runes are primarily a tool for developing the quality of your own perception. Giving that tool away entirely defeats the purpose.

Reading for yourself requires being willing to see what the runes actually say rather than what you want them to say. This is a developed capacity, not an innate one. Early in a practice, it is common to find yourself drawing a rune, feeling disappointed or uncomfortable with it, and immediately drawing another one "to clarify." This is usually wishful thinking in action, and recognizing it as such is itself useful information. The rune that makes you want to draw another one is typically the one you most need to stay with.

A few specific practices help. One is to record the rune before analyzing it — write down what you drew before you begin to interpret it, so that you cannot later misremember having drawn something more comfortable. Another is to wait before interpreting: draw the rune, note it, go about your morning, and return to the interpretation with some distance from the initial reaction. A third is to practice reading for situations you are not personally invested in — questions about public events, historical situations, anything where your preferences are not engaged — as a way of developing the reading capacity without the interference of personal stakes.

Reading for Others

When someone asks you to read runes for them, the situation changes in ways that are worth being clear about. You are no longer the querent; you are the intermediary. Your role is to bring your developed relationship with the runes to bear on someone else's question, and to offer what you perceive with as much accuracy and as little projection as possible.

The most important principle in reading for others is this: you are reporting what the runes show, not what you think the person should hear. These are not always the same thing. The rune that appears may carry a message the person does not want to receive, or may point toward an aspect of their situation that they have been avoiding. Your job is not to protect them from what the runes say or to soften it into something more palatable. It is to communicate clearly what you see, with the care and respect that honest communication requires.

This means paying attention to the distinction between what the runes show and your own interpretation of it. "Hagalaz appeared in the present position, which suggests disruption or significant challenge in the current situation" is a rune reading. "You're going to go through something really difficult" is an interpretation that may or may not follow from the reading. Offering both — the observation and the interpretation — and being clear about which is which, is good practice.

It also means being honest about the limits of what you can see. A spread that is genuinely ambiguous should be described as ambiguous. A reading that raises a question you cannot answer should raise the question openly. The authority of runic divination does not depend on the reader's appearing to know more than they know. It depends on the quality of attention they bring to what actually appears.

Respecting the Tradition

Working with the runes today means working with a tradition that belongs to a specific cultural and historical context — one whose living descendants are real people with ongoing relationships to their own heritage. This is worth naming directly, because the popularity of runes in contemporary spiritual practice has produced some of its most serious misuses alongside some of its most sincere engagement.

The runes are not owned by any single community, and there is no legitimate authority that can grant or withhold permission to work with them. But they carry history — including the deeply troubling appropriation of certain runic symbols by twentieth-century ideological movements whose legacy continues to cause harm. Several Elder Futhark runes, and some younger runic forms, were adopted as insignia by the Nazi SS and by subsequent neo-fascist movements. Bringing this history into awareness is not a reason to avoid the runes. It is a reason to understand them fully enough to distinguish the tradition from its misuse, and to engage with that distinction consciously rather than pretending it does not exist.

Working with the runes with respect for the tradition means engaging with the actual history and mythology, not a romanticized or invented version of it. It means remaining curious rather than certain about meanings and interpretations. It means acknowledging that this is a living tradition, not a fixed system, and that others' relationships with it deserve the same consideration you would want for your own.

The Long Work

A rune practice does not reach a point of completion. There is no level of mastery beyond which the daily rune becomes unnecessary, or the journal redundant, or the meditation on a single symbol unproductive. The tradition is too deep and too complex for any single practitioner to exhaust it, and the work of bringing the runes into contact with a living human life is always new because the life is always changing.

What does change, over time and with sustained practice, is the quality of the relationship. The runes that felt opaque and abstract in the early months become familiar presences with distinctive qualities, recognizable immediately. The readings that produced confusion begin to produce clarity — not because the runes have changed, but because your capacity to hear what they are saying has developed. The daily practice that felt effortful starts to feel natural, and on the days you skip it, you notice its absence in the texture of your attention.

This is what the practice is building toward: not expertise in a technical sense, but a deepened quality of perception that extends beyond the rune bag and into ordinary life. The runes are instruments for developing a particular kind of attention — the attention that can hold complexity without collapsing it into premature certainty, that can sit with what is difficult without flinching, that can recognize pattern and meaning in what appears accidental. These capacities, once developed, do not stay inside the container of a formal practice. They become part of how you move through the world.

That is what Odin was after, hanging from the tree. Not a set of symbols. A way of seeing.

Stones That Speak: The Great Runic Inscriptions

T he runes did not survive only in manuscripts and mythological poems. They survived in stone, in bone, in wood, in metal — in the physical marks left by people who lived and worked and traveled and grieved across a thousand years of Northern European history. These objects are the most direct evidence we have of what the runic tradition actually looked like in practice, and the most significant of them deserve more than a catalog entry. Each one is a document — of a specific moment, a specific community, a specific understanding of what it meant to put a mark on a surface and send it forward into time.

What follows is a close look at seven of the most historically important runic inscriptions: the objects and stones that have contributed most to our understanding of the runes, their use, and the world they came from. They span roughly twelve centuries, from a small antler comb found in a bog to a dense boulder whose meaning scholars are still actively debating.

The Vimose Comb

The oldest securely dated runic inscription comes from a bog deposit at Vimose on the Danish island of Funen, excavated in the nineteenth century. Among the extraordinary collection of weapons, tools, and personal objects deliberately deposited there — a war-offering, most likely, objects taken from a defeated enemy and given to the water — was a small comb carved from antler. On its spine, in clean and confident Elder Futhark letters, is the word *harja*. The inscription dates to around 160 CE.

The word's meaning is not entirely settled. It may be a personal name. It may mean warrior. What is not in question is the quality of the carving: this is the work of someone who knew what they were doing, who had internalized the angular forms of the runic alphabet well enough to cut them into a small curved surface without hesitation. The Vimose comb is not an apprentice piece. It belongs to a tradition that was already mature by the mid-second century — which means the tradition itself is older still, its origins retreating further into a period from which no surviving inscription yet confirms them.

Standing with the comb's image — it is small enough to hold in one hand — it is easy to forget how far it has traveled. The person who carved *harja* into this piece of antler did so roughly eighteen centuries ago, in a community for which we have no written records, in a language that had not yet diverged into the forms that would eventually become Old Norse and Old English and Old High German. The runes on this comb are as old to the Bryggen inscriptions as the Bryggen inscriptions are to us.

The Kylver Stone

The Kylver Stone, a limestone slab discovered built into the wall of a grave in Gotland, Sweden, and dated to around 400 CE, holds the distinction of carrying the first known complete inscription of the Elder Futhark in sequence. All twenty-four runes, in their traditional order, from *fehu* to *othala*, followed by a small bindrune and what appears to be a palindrome of uncertain meaning.

The significance of this object for runic scholarship is considerable: the Kylver Stone is essentially the primary evidence for the canonical sequence of the Elder Futhark, the text from which all subsequent discussions of the correct ordering of the twenty-four runes take their orientation. Without it, the order we work with today would rest on considerably less certain ground.

But the stone's interest goes beyond its scholarly utility. It was found inside a grave — not displayed on a road or erected in a public space, but sealed within the burial of a specific person, oriented with its inscription face down against the body. This placement strongly suggests that the complete futhark was understood to function as a protective inscription, the full set of runic forces present to accompany or guard the dead. The runes here are not communicating information. They are performing a function: the assembled presence of all twenty-four energies, gathered in their proper sequence, holding their power over whatever lay within the stone's compass.

The Kylver Stone is now held at the Museum of National Antiquities in Stockholm. The grave it came from has long since been disturbed, but the stone itself endures — a limestone slab roughly the size of a laptop, carrying on its surface the complete vocabulary of a tradition that would last another fifteen centuries after whoever placed it there had turned to dust.

The Björketorp Runestone

In a field in the Swedish province of Blekinge, three large stones stand in a rough triangle. Two of them are unmarked. The third, the Björketorp Runestone, is nearly four meters tall and carries one of the most deliberately menacing runic inscriptions in the entire corpus. Carved in the Elder Futhark and dated to the late sixth or early seventh century, the text reads, in translation: I, *master of the runes, conceal here runes of power. Ceaselessly tormented by maleficence is he who breaks this monument.*

The stone does not explain what it is marking. Scholars have proposed that it is a grave marker, a territorial boundary, a site of ritual significance, a monument to an event now lost to the record. None of these proposals has achieved consensus. What the inscription does make unambiguously clear is the status the carver claimed: *master of the runes*, a title that asserts specialized knowledge and the authority that goes with it. The warning attached is not metaphorical, at least not in the carver's understanding. The runes concealed within and around the stone were understood as genuinely dangerous forces, and the person who carved them knew how to direct them.

The Björketorp Stone is unusual in the runic corpus not because it uses runes for protection and threat — this was common — but because of its scale and its explicitness. Most protective inscriptions are modest, embedded in objects, not declaring themselves from a monument four meters high in an open field. Whatever the stone marked, whoever commissioned it understood the runes as a technology capable of defending it across centuries, without anyone needing to be present to enforce the warning.

The Jelling Stones

In the small Danish town of Jelling, in the churchyard of a twelfth-century church built on a site of considerably older significance, stand two large runestones. Together they are among the most important surviving monuments of the Viking Age — not only for what they say but for when they were made and what they represent about the moment in which they were made.

The smaller of the two stones was raised by King Gorm the Old in memory of his wife Thyra, sometime in the early tenth century. It is a straightforward memorial inscription, large and well carved but conventional in its form. The larger stone, raised by Gorm's son Harald Bluetooth sometime around 965 CE, is a different kind of object entirely. Its three faces carry an inscription that declares Harald's accomplishments — he unified Denmark, he conquered Norway, he made the Danes Christian — alongside two images: a representation of the great Midgard Serpent entwined with another creature, and an image of Christ rendered in the knotwork style of Norse art, his arms spread in a posture that echoes the crucifixion but whose visual language is entirely Viking Age.

Harald's stone is a monument to a cultural transition written in the language of what it is transitioning away from. A Christian king, at the moment of his conversion, chose runes — the pre-Christian script, the script of the old gods — to announce his new religion to his subjects. The image of Christ is indistinguishable in style from the images that appeared on pagan monuments for generations before it. The stone is neither fully of the old world nor of the new; it exists at the exact threshold between them, which is precisely what it was designed to do — to present the new faith in forms that the old tradition had made authoritative.

The Jelling Stones are now a UNESCO World Heritage Site. They stand outdoors in the same churchyard where they were erected more than a thousand years ago, which means that the stone Harald raised to announce the Christianization of Denmark stands in the shadow of a Christian church built on ground that was already sacred before either stone or church existed. The layers of that continuity are difficult to fully take in.

The Karlevi Runestone

On the small Swedish island of Öland, near the water's edge, stands a runestone that holds a distinction unlike any other in the entire runic corpus: it is the only stone known to carry a complete skaldic verse, inscribed in the densely allusive poetic form known as *dróttkvætt* — the meter of the Viking Age court poets. Erected around 1000 CE, the Karlevi Stone commemorates a man named Sibbi, described as the most capable leader who had ever come to settle on Öland, and the verse on its face praises him in language of extraordinary compression and craft.

Dróttkvætt was among the most demanding poetic forms ever developed in any language: each half-stanza of six syllables had to satisfy simultaneous requirements of alliteration, internal rhyme, and syllable count, and the meaning was typically buried in layers of kenning — metaphorical compound nouns of such density that untangling them requires specialized knowledge even today. A poet who could compose in *dróttkvætt* had undergone years of formal training. That someone chose this form for a runestone inscription — working it out in the angular, space-constrained medium of carved stone — speaks to both the prestige of the poetic tradition and the sophistication of the community that commissioned the monument.

What makes the Karlevi Stone particularly striking in the context of this book is what it reveals about the range of the runic tradition. The same alphabet used to scratch a shopping list on a wooden stick in Bergen was used here to carry some of the most technically demanding poetry the medieval Norse world produced. The runes were not a single register. They were a complete writing system, available across the full spectrum of human expression from the completely mundane to the most formally elaborate.

The Rök Stone

The Rök Stone, standing in a churchyard in the Swedish province of Östergötland, is the longest runic inscription in existence and one of the most intellectually demanding objects in the entire corpus of Old Norse literature. Erected sometime in the ninth century, the stone carries more than seven hundred runes on all five of its surfaces, in a combination of Younger Futhark and several cipher systems — encoded versions of the runic alphabet that required the reader to know not only the letters but the key to the substitution being used.

The inscription is addressed to the memory of a young man named Vámoðr, evidently the son of the person who raised the stone, a man named Varinn. Beyond this basic framework, the text has resisted full interpretation for over a century of scholarly effort. It contains mythological allusions, riddles, references to events that may be historical or legendary or both, and a structure of inquiry and response that reads almost like a ritual text — a series of questions posed to the runes themselves, or perhaps to the assembled dead. Some of the riddles embedded in the stone have been solved after decades of study; others have not.

The sheer density of what Varinn put onto the stone raises questions that the inscription itself does not answer. Why encode parts of the text in cipher, when a memorial stone's purpose is typically public legibility? Who was the intended reader — someone who passed by on a road, or someone who already knew enough to work through the cipher systems? The most plausible answer is that the Rök Stone's audience was not the casual traveler but a specific community of people with deep runic knowledge, for whom the stone functioned as a kind of public demonstration of that knowledge: look how much is contained here, look how deeply the person who raised this stone understood the tradition.

Recent scholarship has proposed a reading of the stone's central concern as a meditation on the fear of a new Fimbulwinter — the great winter that Norse mythology associates with the coming of Ragnarök — triggered by a series of natural phenomena that Varinn's community had recently experienced, including an unusually severe winter, a solar eclipse, and famine. In this reading, the stone is not primarily a memorial but a form of propitiatory magic: an inscription designed to call on the forces the runes represent to ward off a catastrophe that seemed, in the specific historical moment of its carving, to be genuinely approaching. Varinn is not only commemorating his son. He is doing something with the runes — reaching, through the accumulated weight of mythological reference and encoded knowledge, toward forces capable of turning what he fears is coming.

Whether or not this reading is correct, the Rök Stone stands as evidence that the runes were understood, even in the ninth century, as capable of serious intellectual and spiritual work far beyond the commemorative formulas of most runestones. Whoever carved it — and the skill of the carving, the complexity of the systems used, and the density of the mythological reference all point to someone with exceptional runic knowledge — was working at the highest level of what the tradition could do.

The Bryggen Inscriptions

The final objects in this chapter are not monumental. They are, if anything, the opposite: small pieces of wood and bone, roughly cut, their inscriptions casual in a way that grand memorial stones are not. The Bryggen inscriptions, discovered from the 1950s onward in the waterlogged layers beneath Bergen's medieval harbor district, are the largest single body of runic material from the medieval period, and they changed the scholarly understanding of who used runes and how.

More than six hundred inscriptions have been recovered from Bryggen so far, on wooden sticks and flat pieces of bone, dating primarily from the twelfth through fourteenth centuries. The content is overwhelmingly ordinary. Names and addresses — the medieval equivalent of a mailing label. Commercial transactions, debt records, receipts. Personal messages of the kind that might today be sent as a text. Prayers in Latin, written out in runic letters because the writer knew the alphabet but apparently wrote more comfortably in runes than in Roman script. One stick carries an inscription that translates roughly as a declaration of love; another seems to be a list of goods; a third contains what appears to be an off-color joke.

The Bryggen inscriptions are not literature. They are laundry. They are the accumulated detritus of a busy medieval port community, people writing to each other about immediate practical matters, using the runic alphabet as unselfconsciously as we use a keyboard. What they prove is that by the high Middle Ages, well into the Christian era, runic literacy in Norway was not confined to specialists or to sacred use. It was available to merchants, to dock workers, to the people who moved goods in and out of a harbor. The runes had not lost their deeper associations — the same Bergen material includes inscriptions that are clearly magical in character, protective formulas and invocations sitting in the same archive as the shopping lists — but they had also become, or perhaps had always been, simply a way of writing things down.

The Bryggen inscriptions are held at the University of Bergen's Bryggens Museum, where excavation has continued intermittently since their first discovery. Each new dig season has the potential to add to the corpus. The record is not yet complete.

Runes Today: From Revival to the Present

CHAPTER 13

Runes Today: From Revival to the Present

T he runes did not simply survive into the modern world. They were rediscovered, reinterpreted, contested, misappropriated, reclaimed, and are currently in the middle of a revival that is both broader and more diverse than anything that has come before. Understanding where the runes stand today requires tracing a path through roughly two centuries of that history — a path that passes through the Romantic movement, the darkest chapter in the runes' modern story, the counterculture of the 1970s, and the contemporary moment in which millions of people around the world are working with the Elder Futhark in ways ranging from daily meditation to academic scholarship to tattoo art.

The Romantic Rediscovery

By the seventeenth century, runic literacy in Scandinavia had declined to the point where the symbols were no longer widely recognized, even in the regions where they had remained in use longest. The Dalecarlian tradition continued in isolation in the Swedish province of Dalarna, but it was invisible to the wider cultural conversation. Elsewhere, the runes had become curiosities — objects in cabinets, subjects for antiquarian speculation, inscriptions that could be found but not always read.

What changed was Romanticism. The broad cultural movement that swept Europe in the late eighteenth and early nineteenth centuries brought with it an intense interest in the pre-Christian past of the Germanic and Scandinavian peoples, and the runes became one of its primary focal points. Scholars began collecting and publishing runic inscriptions in earnest. The Eddas were translated into modern languages for the first time and read with the excitement of rediscovered treasure. Norse mythology — Odin, Thor, the Nine Worlds, Ragnarök — entered the artistic mainstream of northern Europe, inspiring poetry, painting, opera, and eventually, inevitably, nationalist politics.

In this atmosphere, the runes acquired a new layer of cultural meaning alongside their historical one. They were no longer merely an ancient alphabet; they were symbols of a specific ethnic and cultural heritage, markers of connection to a pre-Christian past that Romantic nationalists constructed with more enthusiasm than accuracy. This construction was not inherently malicious — much of it was simply the normal human process of making meaningful objects from the available materials of history. But the materials were being selected, and the selection had consequences that would become catastrophic in the twentieth century.

The Shadow: Runes Under National Socialism

Any honest account of the runes in the modern world must pass through this territory, because it is still shaping the landscape. In the late nineteenth and early twentieth centuries, a German occultist and self-described runic scholar named Guido von List developed a system he claimed to have received during a period of blindness following eye surgery — a set of eighteen runes he called the Armanen Futhark, which he presented as the original and secret runic system underlying the Elder Futhark. Von List's work was not serious scholarship. It was creative mythology dressed in scholarly language, shaped by the pan-Germanic nationalist ideology that was gaining ground in Austria and Germany in the years before the First World War. But it was enormously influential in certain circles, and the associations it forged between specific runic symbols and ideas of racial identity and national destiny proved durable in ways that had profound consequences.

The Schutzstaffel — the SS — adopted two Sowilo runes as its insignia, the double lightning bolt symbol that became one of the most recognizable emblems of the Nazi state. Other runic symbols were appropriated for use in the iconography of the regime: Tiwaz for an SS division, Othala for another, Lebensrune and Todesrune — the "life rune" and "death rune" derived from Algiz — for the SS's birth and death records. Himmler, who had a deep personal investment in Germanic occultism, was particularly drawn to runic symbolism, and the SS's internal culture made extensive use of it.

The effect of this association on the runes' cultural standing has been long-lasting and serious. In contemporary Germany, several runic symbols remain legally restricted as potential neo-Nazi insignia. In the broader culture, the presence of runic symbols — particularly the Sowilo double flash and the Othala rune — in certain political contexts remains a recognized signal of affiliation with white nationalist ideology. This is not a historical curiosity. It is a current reality, and anyone working with the runes in the contemporary world needs to be aware of it.

The runes themselves are not contaminated by this use any more than a tree is contaminated by having been used to make a weapon.

The symbols predate their twentieth-century appropriation by two thousand years, and the vast majority of people working with them today have no connection whatsoever to the ideology that misused them. But awareness of the history is part of responsible engagement with the tradition — both because it explains why certain symbols require contextual sensitivity, and because the ongoing work of reclaiming the runes' integrity from their appropriation is something the contemporary runic community takes seriously and participates in actively.

The Modern Revival

The contemporary runic revival has several distinct roots, which have grown together over the past half-century into something considerably more diverse and more serious than any of its individual origins.

One root is the Ásatrú movement, which began formally in Iceland in 1972 when Sveinbjörn Beinteinsson received official government recognition for a religious organization devoted to the pre-Christian Norse faith. Ásatrú — the name means, roughly, loyalty to the Æsir gods — spread rapidly to Scandinavia, the United States, and elsewhere through the 1970s and 1980s. For Ásatrú practitioners, the runes are not primarily a divination tool; they are sacred symbols embedded in the cosmology of a living religious tradition, worked with through ritual, study, meditation, and galdr in ways that attempt to maintain continuity with the historical practice. Modern Ásatrú communities vary considerably in their theological and cultural positions, but the runes are nearly universal among them as a central element of practice.

A second root is the broader occult and New Age revival of the 1970s and 1980s, which brought the runes to a much wider audience than the Ásatrú movement alone could reach. Books by Ralph Blum, Edred Thorsson, Freya Aswynn, and others introduced the Elder Futhark to readers who might have no connection to Norse religion but were drawn to the runes as a divination system, a psychological tool, or a form of symbolic meditation. Blum's *The Book of Runes*, published in 1982, sold millions of copies and introduced the runes to an audience for which they became a personal practice completely independent of any formal religious affiliation. This democratization of runic practice came with trade-offs — some of the popular presentations of the runes simplified or distorted the tradition significantly — but it also made the symbols available to many people who have since developed serious and well-informed practices of their own.

Runes in Contemporary Culture

The most visible presence of the runes in contemporary culture is not in spiritual practice but in popular media. The Marvel Cinematic Universe, with its enormously successful Thor and Avengers franchises, has made the names Odin, Thor, Loki, Asgard, and Mjölnir familiar to audiences worldwide who may have no other connection to Norse mythology. This is a double-edged development. On one hand, it has sparked genuine curiosity about the historical and mythological tradition underlying the films — searches for information about actual Norse mythology spike measurably after Marvel releases. On the other hand, the Marvel versions of these figures are so thoroughly transformed by their American superhero context that they bear only a glancing relationship to their source material, and the casual conflation of the two causes genuine confusion.

Video games have been another significant vector. The *God of War* series, beginning with its 2018 entry set in the Norse cosmological world, engaged with Norse mythology with considerable seriousness and craft, driving further interest in the actual tradition. Runic symbols appear throughout the game's visual design, and the attention to mythological accuracy — while selective and adapted for narrative purposes — is evident. Similarly, the *Assassin's Creed: Valhalla* game introduced millions of players to a Viking Age world rendered with significant historical and archaeological research behind it.

Tattoos represent one of the most personal forms of contemporary runic engagement, and runic tattoos have become genuinely widespread over the past two decades. The Elder Futhark, the Younger Futhark, bindrunes, and individual runic symbols appear on people's bodies for reasons ranging from aesthetic to deeply personal to specifically spiritual. This development connects back to an old tradition — the Norse sources mention runic inscription on the body, and the deliberate placement of a permanent runic symbol on your skin is not so different in principle from the inscription of a runic amulet that was meant to remain in close contact with the body. The practice also introduces the same responsibilities that any runic work involves: understanding what you are working with before you commit to it permanently.

Jewelry, home goods, clothing, and decorative objects bearing runic symbols constitute a commercial market of considerable size, and this market encompasses everything from thoughtfully crafted objects made with genuine knowledge of the tradition to mass-produced items that treat the runes as vaguely Scandinavian-looking decoration. This range is not new — the tradition has always included objects made for their symbolic power and objects made for their visual appeal, and the line between the two has never been entirely sharp. What matters, as with all runic work, is the relationship between the person and the symbol: whether the object carrying the rune is held as something meaningful or merely worn as an accessory.

Who Practices Today

The contemporary runic community is not a unified thing. It encompasses Ásatrú practitioners for whom the runes are embedded in a living religious tradition; solitary practitioners working with the Elder Futhark as a personal spiritual and psychological tool; scholars pursuing the academic study of runic inscriptions, Old Norse texts, and the historical practice; artists incorporating runic symbolism into visual and literary work; and many people who occupy multiple of these categories at once.

What these communities share, broadly, is a commitment to taking the runes seriously — to engaging with the tradition's depth rather than treating the symbols as decorative. There is ongoing, sometimes heated, debate within the community about what that seriousness requires: how closely modern practice needs to track historical evidence, what role personal and intuitive engagement can legitimately play alongside academic study, how to manage the tension between accessibility and rigor, and how to address the ongoing challenge of the tradition's association with far-right ideology.

The last question deserves its own brief attention, because it is one that responsible practitioners cannot avoid. The same symbols used by millions of people worldwide as tools for meditation, divination, and spiritual practice appear in the insignia of white nationalist organizations. The response of most of the contemporary runic community is neither to abandon the symbols nor to pretend the association does not exist, but to continue working visibly and openly with the tradition in its full historical and cultural complexity — producing scholarship, practice, and community that demonstrates, by example and by explicit statement, that the runes belong to a tradition that vastly predates any nationalist appropriation and that is available, in principle, to any person of any background who approaches it with genuine respect and seriousness.

This reclamation is ongoing. It will not be complete until the symbols are so thoroughly associated with serious, inclusive, well-grounded practice that their misuse becomes the anomaly rather than the association. The people doing this work — practitioners, scholars, artists, teachers — are contributing to something larger than their individual practices. They are participating in the long process by which the runes, having survived everything from the Christian-ization of Scandinavia to the Nazi appropriation of the twentieth century, are finding their way back to what they have always been: a set of ancient symbols pointing toward the forces that structure existence, available to anyone willing to pay the cost that serious engagement with them has always required.

Odin paid nine days on the World Tree. The runes are worth con-siderably less than that. But they do ask for something — attention, honesty, consistency, the willingness to sit with what you do not yet understand. The tradition's survival across two thousand years of upheaval suggests that this is a reasonable price, and that what the runes offer in return is worth the paying.

Conclusion

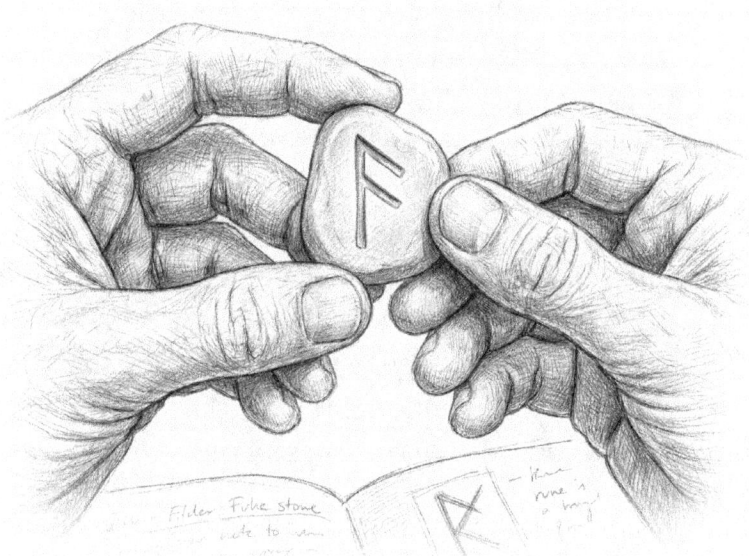

I'm back in Norway as I write this. Different trip, different purpose — no archives, no family research this time, just the landscape and the long northern light. But I find myself thinking, as I often do here, about that first encounter with the runes in a small museum more years ago than I want to count. The angular marks on the stone. The feeling of recognition that I couldn't account for.

I understand that feeling somewhat better now, though not completely. I'm not sure I ever will, and I've stopped expecting to. The runes are built that way — they hold more than you can hold at once, and the part that exceeds your current capacity is exactly where the work is. Every practitioner I've spoken with over the years has described some version of the same experience: you think you understand a rune, and then it shows you something else, something you weren't ready to see the last time you looked. This is not a sign that you've been wrong. It's a sign that the practice is working.

What I hope this book has given you is a foundation — not a finished structure, but the kind of ground that can support one. The history matters because it shows you what the runes actually were, as opposed to what anyone has claimed they were, and that knowledge protects you from the worst of the distortions that accumulate around any tradition that people care about passionately. The mythology matters because the runes grew from that world, and you cannot fully understand a symbol without understanding the story it came from. The twenty-four rune descriptions matter as a starting vocabulary, a set of orientations that will become your own over time as you work with them and they work on you.

But the part that matters most is the part that only you can do: the daily draw, the notebook, the patient accumulation of a relationship with these symbols across the specific and unrepeatable conditions of your own life. That is where the runes become real rather than theoretical. That is where they stop being a system you are learning and become a practice you are living.

A few things I've found to be reliably true, for whatever they're worth.

The runes are honest. They do not tell you what you want to hear. Over time, if you keep a careful record of your readings and return to them at intervals, you will find that the runes were more accurate than you gave them credit for — that what seemed obscure or unhelpful at the time was pointing at something that only became visible later. This can be unsettling in retrospect, but it is also one of the things that builds genuine trust in the practice.

The runes are patient. You can put the notebook down for a month and come back, and they will receive you without reproach. The tradition has survived two thousand years and several serious attempts to erase or misuse it. It does not need you to be perfect. It needs you to return.

The runes ask for honesty in return. The readings that have served me best have been the ones where I was able to set down my pre-ferred version of the situation and ask the runes what was actually there. This is harder than it sounds. We are all, to some degree, invested in our own narratives. The practice of drawing a rune each morning and sitting with it before you've decided what the day means is a small but consistent practice in the opposite direction — in remaining open to what is rather than confirming what you've already concluded.

And finally: the runes are connected to something larger than any single practitioner's experience of them. The tradition flows back-ward through centuries of use, through carvers and völvas and merchants and scholars and farmers who put marks on wood and stone for purposes ranging from the entirely mundane to the deeply sacred. When you work with these symbols, you are participating in that continuity — not passively, but as one more person who found something worth taking seriously in a set of ancient marks and decided to pay the cost of serious engagement.

Odin hung nine days on the tree. The runes came up to meet him.

Whatever road brought you to this book, I hope the runes meet you too.

References

T he following works informed the research and writing of this book. They are organized thematically to allow readers to pursue particular areas of interest. Where multiple editions exist, the most widely available is noted.

Primary Sources

The two foundational texts for anyone studying Norse mythology and runic tradition are the Poetic Edda and the Prose Edda. Several reliable translations are available in English.

Crawford, Jackson. *The Poetic Edda: Stories of the Norse Gods and Heroes*. Hackett Publishing, 2015. A readable modern translation with useful introductory material, particularly strong on the *Hávamál*.

Hollander, Lee M. *The Poetic Edda*. University of Texas Press, 1962. The standard scholarly translation for most of the twentieth century, with detailed notes.

Larrington, Carolyne. *The Poetic Edda*. Oxford University Press, 2014 (revised edition). The Oxford World's Classics translation, widely used in academic contexts.

Byock, Jesse. *The Prose Edda*. Penguin Classics, 2005. A clear and accessible translation of Snorri Sturluson's thirteenth-century compilation, with a useful introduction to its historical context.

Faulkes, Anthony. *Edda* (Snorri Sturluson). Everyman, 1987. The standard scholarly English translation of the Prose Edda.

Fell, Christine, et al., trans. *Egil's Saga*. Penguin Classics, 1976. The saga referenced in Chapter 9, containing the famous account of Egil's runic intervention.

Mattingly, H., and S.A. Handford, trans. *Tacitus: The Agricola and the Germania*. Penguin Classics, 1970. Contains the passage on Germanic divination practices discussed in Chapter 1.

Norse Mythology and Religion

Abram, Christopher. *Myths of the Pagan North: The Gods of the Norsemen*. Continuum, 2011. A scholarly but accessible survey of the sources and their limitations.

Davidson, H.R. Ellis. *Gods and Myths of Northern Europe*. Penguin, 1964. Still one of the clearest general introductions to the Norse pantheon and its religious context.

Davidson, H.R. Ellis. *The Road to Hel: A Study of the Conception of the Dead in Old Norse Literature*. Cambridge University Press, 1943. Dated in some respects but valuable on Norse understandings of death and the afterlife.

Lindow, John. *Norse Mythology: A Guide to the Gods, Heroes, Rituals, and Beliefs*. Oxford University Press, 2001. A comprehensive reference work organized encyclopedically by entry.

Simek, Rudolf. *Dictionary of Northern Mythology*. Translated by Angela Hall. D.S. Brewer, 1993. The most thorough single-volume reference on Norse mythological figures, places, and concepts.

Orchard, Andy. *Dictionary of Norse Myth and Legend*. Cassell, 1997. A useful companion to Simek, with somewhat more accessible prose.

Price, Neil. *Children of Ash and Elm: A History of the Vikings*. Basic Books, 2020. The most comprehensive recent synthesis of Viking Age history and culture, drawing on decades of archaeological research.

Runic Studies

Barnes, Michael P. *Runes: A Handbook*. Boydell Press, 2012. The most rigorous and up-to-date general introduction to runic studies available in English, covering all the major futharks and their historical contexts.

Elliott, Ralph W.V. *Runes: An Introduction*. Manchester University Press, 1959. An older but still useful introduction to the Elder Futhark and its archaeological context.

Looijenga, Tineke. *Texts and Contexts of the Oldest Runic Inscriptions*. Brill, 2003. The most thorough scholarly treatment of the earliest runic material, including the Meldorf fibula and the Vimose corpus.

Page, R.I. *An Introduction to English Runes*. Methuen, 1973. The standard reference on the Anglo-Saxon Futhorc tradition.

Page, R.I. *Runes*. British Museum Press, 1987. A concise, well-illustrated introduction to the runic tradition as a whole, produced in connection with the British Museum's collection.

Spurkland, Terje. *Norwegian Runes and Runic Inscriptions*. Translated by Betsy van der Hoek. Boydell Press, 2005. The most detailed treatment in English of the Norwegian runic corpus, including the Bryggen inscriptions.

Antonsen, Elmer H. *A Concise Grammar of the Older Runic Inscriptions*. Max Niemeyer Verlag, 1975. A technical linguistic study, recommended for readers with a background in historical linguistics.

Viking Age Archaeology and History

Byock, Jesse. *Viking Age Iceland*. Penguin, 2001. An authoritative account of Icelandic society in the Viking Age, with extensive material on the legal and social structures within which the runic tradition operated.

Jesch, Judith. *Women in the Viking Age*. Boydell Press, 1991. Includes important material on female runic practitioners and female-commissioned runestones.

Jesch, Judith. *The Viking Diaspora*. Routledge, 2015. A survey of the geographic spread of Norse culture and its material remains, including runic inscriptions.

Price, Neil. *The Viking Way: Magic and Mind in Late Iron Age Scandinavia*. Oxbow Books, 2002 (second edition, 2019). The definitive scholarly study of Norse magical practice, seidr, and the archaeological evidence for shamanism. Essential reading for anyone interested in the material covered in Chapter 9.

Modern Runic Practice

Aswynn, Freya. *Northern Mysteries and Magick: Runes and Feminine Powers*. Llewellyn, 1998. One of the most serious and historically grounded of the modern practical guides to runic work.

Thorsson, Edred (Stephen Flowers). *Futhark: A Handbook of Rune Magic*. Weiser Books, 1984. Influential in the modern revival; readers should note that Thorsson's interpretive framework is his own construction rather than a direct recovery of historical practice, but the book is serious in its engagement with the sources.

Paxson, Diana L. *Taking Up the Runes: A Complete Guide to Using Runes in Spells, Rituals, Divination, and Magic*. Weiser Books, 2005. A thorough practical guide by one of the more historically careful modern practitioners.

A Note to the Reader

If this book has been useful to you — if it has given you a clearer sense of where the runes come from, what they mean, and how to begin working with them — I would be genuinely grateful if you took a few minutes to leave a review on Amazon.

Reviews make an enormous difference for independent authors. They help other readers find the book, and they help me understand what is resonating and what could be better. A sentence or two about what you found valuable is more than enough. Your words carry more weight than you might expect.

Thank you for spending time with the runes, and with this book. I hope it is the beginning of a long and rewarding practice.

Erik Hansen

www.ingramcontent.com/pod-product-compliance
Lightning Source LLC
Chambersburg PA
CBHW071753120626

46550CB00002B/781